# THE UNFORGIVABLE SIN

# THE UNFORGIVABLE SIN

*Spiritual Formation Through Forgiveness,
Repentance, and Reconciliation*

## Mikal J. Shedd

# THE UNFORGIVABLE SIN
## SPIRITUAL FORMATION THROUGH FORGIVENESS, REPENTANCE, AND RECONCILIATION

Copyright © 2017 Mikal J. Shedd.

All rights reserved. No part of this book may be used or reproduced by any means, graphic, electronic, or mechanical, including photocopying, recording, taping or by any information storage retrieval system without the written permission of the author except in the case of brief quotations embodied in critical articles and reviews.

Unless otherwise noted, all Bible quotations contained herein are from the New Revised Standard Version (NRSV) Bible, copyright 1989, by the Division of Christian Education of the National Council of Churches of Christ in the U. S. A. Used by permission. All rights reserved.

iUniverse books may be ordered through booksellers or by contacting:

iUniverse
1663 Liberty Drive
Bloomington, IN 47403
www.iuniverse.com
1-800-Authors (1-800-288-4677)

Because of the dynamic nature of the Internet, any web addresses or links contained in this book may have changed since publication and may no longer be valid. The views expressed in this work are solely those of the author and do not necessarily reflect the views of the publisher, and the publisher hereby disclaims any responsibility for them.

Any people depicted in stock imagery provided by Thinkstock are models, and such images are being used for illustrative purposes only.
Certain stock imagery © Thinkstock.

ISBN: 978-1-5320-3517-3 (sc)
ISBN: 978-1-5320-3516-6 (e)

Print information available on the last page.

iUniverse rev. date: 11/21/2017

# Contents

Introduction ................................................................. vii

Follow Me ...................................................................... 1
Humble Yourself ......................................................... 10
The Sensation of God's Love ..................................... 17
The Price of Unforgiveness ........................................ 22
The Deal Breaker ........................................................ 28
The Cycle of Unforgiveness ....................................... 36
Breaking the Cycle ..................................................... 43
Cycle of Forgiveness .................................................. 47
Principalities and Powers .......................................... 54
Obstacles to Forgiveness ........................................... 62
Obstacles to Repentance ........................................... 69
Other Issues Interfering with Forgiveness and Repentance ... 79
Reconciliation ............................................................ 83
What We Must Do ..................................................... 88

Appendix A ................................................................. 93
Appendix B ................................................................. 99
Bibliography ............................................................. 127
About the Author ..................................................... 129

# Introduction

Appendix A contains key scriptures used in this book and recommended for meditation.

Instructions for all the prayer forms mentioned in this book are contained in Appendix B.

> *"To forgive the incessant provocations of daily life – to keep on forgiving the bossy mother-in-law, the bullying husband, the nagging wife, the selfish daughter, the deceitful son – how can we do it? Only, I think, by remembering where we stand, by meaning our words when we say in our prayers each night, 'Forgive our trespasses as we forgive those who trespass against us.' We are offered forgiveness on no other terms. To refuse it is to refuse God's mercy for ourselves. There is no hint of exceptions and God means what he says."*
> C.S. Lewis

I have heard it said one has not truly forgiven or repented if one has not reconciled with the other party. Others say if one remembers the offense, one has not truly forgiven.

There is something missing from these interpretations of the process of reconciliation. Reconciliation requires a commitment of both forgiveness and repentance. Separately, forgiveness and repentance are acts of preparation for the process of reconciliation. At any one time, you only have control over half the process. Forgiving is not about forgetting. It is about remembering differently; it is about transforming that memory through the life-giving healing of the Holy Spirit.

It somehow made it easier to forgive when I realized I didn't have to stay near someone who was abusive. All I had to do was forgive; which, in essence, is releasing the situation to God. Couched within that process is the awareness we are also turning ourselves over to God for healing. Until both parties truly make this release, there can be no healing of the relationship. God does not require we subject ourselves to the machinations of abuse in order to reconcile.

Making this release could include anything from a simple, heartfelt apology to getting professional help or even making restitution for our transgressions. Anyone who constantly mistreats or abuses you, then makes excuses for their behavior or apologizes only to do it again does need forgiveness. However, nobody needs to continue in a toxic relationship until both parties have accepted responsibility for their actions or inactions in the situation.

Realize forgiveness and repentance are dependent on accepting responsibility for our lives. Unless we accept responsibility for our lives, all our thoughts, all our decisions, and all our actions; there is no possibility of reconciliation and our forgiveness and our repentance are without meaning. We become mere victims of a cycle of continuously hurting each other.

Of equal importance is the need to grieve as part of the process of forgiving and repenting. What are we grieving for? Grieving is the sign we are taking responsibility for our lives and our actions. It is the sign that on some level we realize what has been lost by this injury. It is a sign we empathize with the other person, beginning to understand the full ramifications of our actions. If we do not make space for the grieving—grieving the lost relationship, what might have been—we will never be able to enter into the process of reconciliation. What is important is being engaged with God for healing from the precipitating event. With God, the desire to do good while engaged in the attempt to heal is what counts. Even if that healing is not completed during our life on this earth.

The following two scriptures inform this book:

> *"For God so loved the world that he gave his only Son, so that everyone who believes in him may not perish but may have eternal life. Indeed, God did*

*not send the Son into the world to condemn the world, but in order that the world might be saved through him." John 3:16-17*

*"He [Jesus] said to him, '"You shall love the Lord your God with all your heart, and with all your soul, and with all your mind.' This is the greatest and first commandment. And a second is like it: 'You shall love your neighbor as yourself.' On these two commandments hang all the law and the prophets." Matthew 22:37-40*

<u>Using this book</u>

At the end of each chapter are Exercises useful for engaging with each lesson. They also help you learn the many methods of prayer available to you. I encourage you to try these exercises, even though they might be unfamiliar to you. By meeting with God on different levels, we lay open our entire mind, body, and spirit to God. You may find yourself astonished by the power a seemingly simple prayer such as the Jesus Prayer can bring into your life. This is an ancient prayer form from the earliest days of Christian prayer practice and is still used to this day because of its powerful way of connecting with God. It is especially powerful when you don't know what to pray. These prayer forms allow room for the Spirit to pray through you and God to answer as we are assured by Romans 8:26-27:

*"Likewise the Spirit helps us in our weakness; for we do not know how to pray as we ought, but that very Spirit intercedes with sighs too deep for words. And God, who searches the heart, knows what is the mind of the Spirit, because the Spirit[s] intercedes for the saints according to the will of God."*

These prayer forms make room for the fulfillment of this promise.

Make it a practice to keep a journal or notepad and pens, pencils, markers, colored pencils, or whatever artistic medium speaks to you.

near you while you pray. This way you will not have to leave your prayer setting to make any notes. I keep a journal and review it at the end of each month and year. It is amazing to see how much I've changed over the past year and I can see how much closer I've progressed towards God. What irritated me last year, does not irritate me today. What irritates me today, will not irritate me next year.

What is being promoted in this book is prayer that places faith in and expects God's action in our lives and in the world. Prayer that is as responsive as it is comforting. Practice these prayers with the expectation of receiving a response and intention to act on any instruction you might receive. If you do this, God will respond. God knows when you are hearing and obeying.

How will you know the response you receive is from God? Jesus gave us the answer to this question in Matthew 22:34-40:

> "When the Pharisees heard that he had silenced the Sadducees, they gathered together, and one of them, a lawyer, asked him a question to test him. 'Teacher, which commandment in the law is the greatest?' He said to him, "You shall love the Lord your God with all your heart, and with all your soul, and with all your mind.' This is the greatest and first commandment. And a second is like it: 'You shall love your neighbor as yourself.' On these two commandments hang all the law and the prophets.'"

Any response you think might come from God will be obedient to either or both of these commandments. Any response you receive that violates one of these commandments is not from God. It is stated, clearly, in I John 4:19-21:

> "We love because he first loved us. Those who say, "I love God," and hate their brothers or sisters, are liars; for those who do not love a brother or sister whom they have seen, cannot love God whom they have not seen. The commandment we have from him is this: those who love God must love their brothers and sisters also."

## Exercises

- Practice Lectio Divina on the following scripture to determine whether you are keeping the two greatest commandments in your life:

  *"Finally, beloved, whatever is true, whatever is honorable, whatever is just, whatever is pure, whatever is pleasing, whatever is commendable, if there is any excellence and if there is anything worth of praise, think about these things." Philippians 4:8*

- Meditate on an offense you have suffered and the action you were planning to take in response to it. Ask yourself the following questions drawn from this scripture:
    - Is it good?
    - Is it loving?
    - Is it healing?
    - Is it faith-filled?
    - Is it true?
    - Is it freeing for all?
    - Will it bring peace to this situation without condoning bad habits or actions?
        - God is in the response if you can answer these questions truthfully with "Yes!"
        - "No!" would indicate your source of direction is not of God.

# Follow Me

"As [Jesus] walked by the Sea of Galilee, he saw two brothers, Simon, who is called Peter, and Andrew his brother, casting a net into the sea—for they were fishermen. And he said to them, 'Follow me, and I will make you fish for people.' Immediately they left their nets and followed him.

"As he went from there, he saw two other brothers, James son of Zebedee and his brother John, in the boat with their father Zebedee, mending their nets, and he called them. Immediately they left the boat and their father, and followed him. Matthew 4:18-22

As we begin the process of forgiving and repenting, there are some important characteristics we need to consider. Because of the grounding of this book in Christianity, one basic assumption this book makes is: you are called to be a follower of Christ.

God calls all people where they are. Since the time of Adam and Eve, God calls us where we are. God called Abraham, Isaac, and Jacob in the midst of their weaknesses. In fact, God knows our weaknesses better than we do.

God called Moses where he was…God did not need Moses to tell him he was not a good speaker, but finally gave in and helped him with his insecurity. Who knows what blessings might have been his if only Moses had said, "Yes!" from the start.

And who can forget the powerful vision in Isaiah 6:1-8?

> "In the year that King Uzziah died, I saw the Lord sitting on a throne, high and lofty; and the hem of his robe filled the temple. Seraphs were in attendance above him; each had six wings: with two they covered their faces, and with two they covered their feet, and with two they flew.
>
> "And one called to another and said: 'Holy, holy, holy is the Lord of hosts; the whole earth is full of his glory. The pivots on the thresholds shook at the voices of those who called, and the house filled with smoke.
>
> "And I said: 'Woe is me! I am lost, for I am a man of unclean lips, and I live among a people of unclean lips; yet my eyes have seen the King, the Lord of hosts!'
>
> "Then one of the seraphs flew to me, holding a live coal that had been taken from the altar with a pair of tongs. The seraph touched my mouth with it and said: 'Now that this has touched your lips, your guilt has departed and your sin is blotted out.'
>
> "Then I heard the voice of the Lord saying, 'Whom shall I send, and who will go for us?' And I said, 'Here am I; send me!'"

Please note: God does not call Isaiah by name here. Isaiah overhears the question and responds. The question itself could have been addressed to any of us and probably is!

Calling is not just a once in a lifetime deal. God calls us many times over our lifespan. The disciples of Jesus were actually re-called after they had followed him for a time. In John 6, Jesus speaks of his followers needing to drink his blood and eat his flesh. This is before the Last

Supper would give such a statement context and many of his disciples left him. At this point, Jesus checks in with his disciples once more:

> *"Because of this many of his disciples turned back and no longer went about with him. So Jesus asked the twelve, 'Do you also wish to go away? Simon Peter answered him, 'Lord, to whom can we go? You have the words of eternal life.'" John 6:66-68*

A second call. A second chance to either refuse or rededicate, now that they knew more about what it meant to follow Christ.

I received a Blessing right after I got my Bachelor's Degree in Accounting. It said I had prepared for a certain vocation in life and that was good. Over the years, I've been called in several ways to serve God, most of them were in some way associated with accounting, but also carried growth-inducing challenges for me. I was called to further my education in order to become a minister. Those degrees came in miraculous ways while I held down a full-time job in accounting.

When I was made aware I had an increased responsibility to priesthood ministry, I asked for it not to come. I just didn't want to deal with it. "There is too much going on in my life, Lord. Being a priest is enough for me right now. Thank-you very much." I prayed it just as if I didn't think God knew what I was dealing with or my capacity to handle something else! I call this a Moses response.

There was even a time when the thought of being a Bishop made me cringe. "Thank-you, but I think I've challenged the bastions of male dominance enough for one lifetime…I'll just stay where I am for now."

One of my biggest concerns with the call to Bishop may seem silly to some, but I knew Bishops had to be able to confront people, to make and uphold decisions that might be unpopular. I had never been able to confront people, at least, not without crying and didn't like to stand firm behind unpopular decisions, rarely sharing my real opinions with others.

My first task following my ordination was to confront the chairperson of a church affiliated organization who had violated the terms of a contract, completely out of ignorance of those terms. She had allowed someone she saw as more knowledgeable than herself to interpret the contract for her. However, he had actually advised her based on assumptions he had made about the contract without actually reading it, either. The contracted firm was threatening us with a breach of contract suit. I spoke with the firm's representative, explaining what happened and getting the information the Board of Directors needed to make a decision on how to repair the situation. I was able to get the Board's decision and settle the matter without a lawsuit.

I had no problem handling the situation. In fact, I didn't even realize I was standing firm until the problem was resolved. That experience left me braver in accepting future calls.

There have been other calls. Some of which I did not recognize to be calls at all. The scriptures are peppered with such calls:

- There was the 'The rich young ruler' in Matthew 19:21-22:

    "Jesus said to him, 'If you wish to be perfect, go, sell your possessions, and give the money to the poor, and you will have treasure in heaven; then come, follow me.' When the young man heard this word, he went away grieving, for he had many possessions."

- And 'The scribe' in Matthew 8:18-20:

    "Now when Jesus saw great crowds around him, he gave orders to go over to the other side. A scribe then approached and said, 'Teacher, I will follow you wherever you go.' And Jesus said to him' "Foxes have holes, and birds of the air have nests; but the Son of Man has nowhere to lay his head.'"

- And, of course, 'The bereaved son' in Matthew 8:21-22:

    "Another of his disciples said to him, 'Lord, first let me go and bury my father.' But Jesus said to him, 'Follow me, and let the dead bury their own dead.'"

In all of these instances, Jesus seems to be saying, "I know you believe you want to follow me, but these are the things that will hold you back." Then he lists for each of them their main obstructions: greed, the need for control and security, and his attachment to family over God's call.

We are all familiar with these kinds of calls and we have all had them in one form or another:

- Calls for accepting the idea that all are called even to the priesthood,
- The call to be more open and less fearful of others who are not like ourselves,
- The call to be generous with those who are struggling because of negative categorizations and judgments built into our culture.
- And then there are the daily calls to follow Christ:
    o Calls to forgive
    o Calls to repent
    o Calls to reach out to someone we would have preferred not to notice.

We have all lost fellowship with friends, even family, because we or they could not respond to these calls.

Yet, the wonder of being a follower of Christ is…Jesus never gives up on us. Jesus always give us a chance to grow into our calls just as he assisted Moses.

Sometimes, we blow past these calls without even noticing we were confronted with a choice. We lost the choice in the morass of our cultural biases. Our habits of thought kept us from seeing there was a choice at all. We were too busy working, playing video games, watching television, or texting. Or, maybe, we were too lazy to check facts just accepted the statements and decisions of those we saw as more knowledgeable then ourselves. It will take something life rending to make us aware we have even been presented with a choice in such situations.

We all know how Simon Peter denied knowing Christ three times because he feared for his life. Not only that, but he did it within hours of swearing to Jesus he would die for him. Peter did not even notice he had done it until the cock crow reminded him of Jesus' words. Then, he wept, bitterly.

But Jesus knew what was needed and called him again, once for each of the denials Peter made:

> "When they had finished breakfast, Jesus said to Simon Peter, 'Simon son of John, do you love me more than these?' He said to him, 'Yes, Lord; you know that I love you.' Jesus said to him, 'Feed my lambs.'
>
> "A second time he said to him, 'Simon son of John, do you love me?' He said to him, 'Yes, Lord; you know that I love you.' Jesus said to him, 'Tend my sheep.'
>
> "He said to him the third time, 'Simon son of John, do you love me?' Peter felt hurt because he said to him the third time, 'Do you love me?' And he said to him, 'Lord, you know everything; you know that I love you.' Jesus said to him, 'Feed my sheep.'"
> John 21: 15-17

The thing we tend to forget about scripture is: it teaches us how God works with His people. We are all called where we are: The proud. The insecure. The angry. The happy. The girl. The boy. The man. The woman. The senior. The junior. The member. The non-member. The Jew. The Muslim. The Buddhist. The Hindu. (Yes, even them!)

We are all called. To ways that stretch us. Grow us. Bring us closer to God. We are all called according to the gifts God has given us. Even............when we don't know we have those gifts to share. Just as I did not know I had it in me to take a stand, God did know and asked me to trust Him on that.

How do we know this? The scriptures are replete with calls to those outside of Israel, outside of the Christian community. Jesus lineage in Matthew 1 is a good illustration of how God calls many people without concern for what or who they are. We have Perez, the son of the incestuous relationship between Judah and his daughter-in-law, Tamar. Then we have Rahab an Amorite and prostitute in Jericho. Rahab is followed closely by Ruth, a Moabite. Then we have Bathsheba, whose husband was killed by David lest someone learn of their adultery. Then we have King Uzziah who turned his back on God and was stricken with leprosy when he tried to make an offering to the Lord without the priests.

Add to this, all of the countries God called to punish and set free the Israelites: the Philistines, Babylon, Cyrus of Persia…so many called, so many chosen. Then we have Peter and Paul, opening baptism to the Gentiles. We are all called.

Here is another calling; a calling laid upon the hearts of each and every one of us. We find this call in Micah 6:8:

> *"He has told you, O mortal, what is good; and what does the Lord require of you but to do justice, and to love kindness (in some versions it reads mercy), and to walk humbly with your God?"*

Intertwined within all of our other calls, we are all called to stand for justice, be kind or merciful, and walk humbly with God as we respond.

This last call is essential to keep in mind. It is echoed in Christ's statement concerning the most important commandments: to love God and our neighbor as ourselves (Matthew 22:37-39). Anytime we are about to embark on a project or an action, we would do well to ask ourselves the following questions:

- Is it just?
- Is it kind (merciful)?
- Am I walking in humility before God?

Is God calling you to something? Something you are having trouble wrapping your mind around? Maybe you think you are not a good speaker…like Moses… Or maybe you have too much to do. You hear the call and know it to be true, but say to yourself, "I will do it when I get the time." Or, maybe it is something too simple…maybe you think it is too demeaning and you could do much more. Or, maybe you are being called to forgive something you consider unforgivable or repent for something you did which you believe you had the right to do. Maybe, you are acting out of fear and the call of God is to be just, be kind, and trust Him anyway. The "walk humbly" part is important to remember at this point.

Stop. Take time to check your perceptions and beliefs concerning the call. Ask yourself questions: Is this a true calling? Do your doubts concern your ability to handle the task at hand or do they seem to come from someplace deeper? Then pray for the answers. If you are sincere in your search, the answers will come. You can even request a sign the call is truly from God. God is good at giving us signs.

Many years ago, when I was still a priest, I was at a priesthood gathering. At one of the meetings, a young man was sitting next to me who, before we had said much more then hello, was telling me all about his relationship with Jesus: his whole spiritual life's story, BAM!, right there. When he was done, he asked me about my story.

I sat quietly for a moment then asked him, "You wouldn't be a missionary by any chance, would you?"

He jumped, then sat there, dumbfounded for a second. Then he said, "I have been longing for some greater way to serve God. I have felt the call, but wasn't sure if it was for me. I asked God to give me a sign at this event this week. I've been a priest for a long time so it's kind of a big step for me. How did you know?"

My response, "You just talk with the courage and conviction of a missionary."

Back to Isaiah: I believe I am not alone in thinking, "If I found myself in the throne room of God with angels flying all over praising God and that hot coal thing touching my lips, I would know I was called, too." But even then, Isaiah had doubts as to his worthiness to even be in that place. He saw himself as lost. Very few people are called with a vision as Isaiah was. If Isaiah could doubt in such a situation, how could we not doubt in our own situation?

But still. We are all called. Even today, God calls us. Can your heart hear God's still, small voice, "Whom shall we send? Who will go for us?"

Do not be afraid to answer the call. You are about to become more than you ever dreamed possible.

## Exercises

Get your journal or a notepad and a pen, setting them where you can reach them during the following meditations. Continue this practice for all subsequent exercises.

- Using the Visualization Practice, review the call of Isaiah 6:1-8. Then answer the following questions:
    - What part did you play in the scripture? Were you a spectator? An angel? Were you Isaiah? Were you as yourself the recipient of the call?
    - How did you feel?
    - How did you respond to the call?
    - How did that feel?
- Memorize or copy Micah 6:8 onto notecards and take it with you as your guide in each decision you make this week. Use it as a daily walking meditation.
    - At the end of each day, use the Consciousness Examen to recap in your journal your experiences each day. Ask yourself the following questions:
        - How did this scripture from Micah change my interactions with others?
        - How did it change how I understood the actions of others?
        - Did my understanding of what constitutes justice change?
    - At the end of the week, review your notes from the week.
        - Do you notice any difference in your response to God's call between the beginning of the week and the end of the week?
        - What were those changes?

# Humble Yourself

"[Jesus] also told this parable to some who trusted in themselves that they were righteous and regarded others with contempt:

"'Two men went up to the temple to pray, one a Pharisee and the other a tax collector. The Pharisee, standing by himself, was praying thus, 'God, I thank you that I am not like other people: thieves, rogues, adulterers, or even like this tax collector. I fast twice a week; I give a tenth of all my income.'

"But the tax collector, standing far off, would not even look up to heaven, but was beating his breast and saying, 'God, be merciful to me, a sinner!'

"I tell you, this man went down to his home justified rather than the other; for all who exalt themselves will be humbled, but all who humble themselves will be exalted." Luke 18:9-14

A fundamental trait of a forgiving and repentant soul is humility. If we are to walk humbly with our God, we must be truly repentant and constantly remember we, too, are forgiven by God.

*The Unforgivable Sin*

When I was laid off recently. I was seriously considering retirement. I attended a retirement seminar to assist me in making that decision. It was meant to help the attendees look at things we may not have considered about retirement or maybe even been afraid to look at. One part of that class was a questionnaire designed to help you analyze your "retirement personality" so you could decide what would be the best retirement activity for you. One of those questions stumped me. It read: "Are you humble? Yes or No?"

The answer I wanted to give was: "I would like to think I was." But "Yes or No?" If I answered "Yes," that could mean I'm not humble. If I answered "No," that could mean I was. I felt like I was being asked to tell them I was either the Pharisee or the tax collector. I did not feel anyone could be a good judge of that trait in themselves. It seemed to me a question better answered by a friend then by me.

The other people at my table told me I was overthinking the question, but the class leaders found it philosophically amusing and said it was a good question, but for the purpose of the questionnaire, to just put "Yes."

While I appreciated their vote of confidence, I realized this was a question I had been dealing with since my early 20s.

When I was around 24, I took a class called "A Prayer Adventure." I can date my true spiritual awakening to the importance of prayer from this class. It was life changing for me in many ways, but the class on humility left me with many questions. Our teacher began the class with her favorite definition of humility: "A candle burning at noon day." (Sandy Bunten) I wrote it down eagerly, being very appreciative of poetic definitions at the time. However, after much reflection, I have since thrown it out. It seemed to me a better definition of pride then of humility.

A number of years later, I was at a retreat when the retreat leader offered what I thought was a much better definition of humility: "Not having a clear picture of how others see you." (Ron Livingston)

I found this definition useful for many years, but came to see it as a little one-sided. While addressing the issues of vanity and self-promotion, it does not address those interior habits of thought that others do not see. I'm sure many of the Pharisee's friends would have labeled him as humble, because this is the "clear picture" the Pharisee tried to convey, but he obviously was not humble. People probably saw the tax collector as very proud indeed, but they, too, would have been wrong.

So, with the definition slate wiped clean before us, let's look at this trait the scriptures call "humility."

In praying about what constitutes humility, I came to realize it was a very complex issue, involving many different layers of being in the world. Instead of definitions, I began to come up with a list of questions. Questions that, when answered, "Yes" would indicate an advanced stage of humility. In case you are wondering, I have had difficulty answering appropriately to all these questions at different times in my life and still do.

The first question has to do with that enigmatic definition, "Not having a clear picture of how others see you."

Are you concerned about how others see you or do you act on God's call without that thought coming into your head? For instance, I spend way too much time picking out what I am wearing to answer that one, "Yes." In fact, I've even been known not to go places because I couldn't decide what to wear!

The second question is like the first: Do you judge yourself and others based on cultural standards of normal? Is someone too black, too brown, too white, too short, too tall, too fat, too thin, dressed inappropriately, handicapped in some way, acting strangely, talking funny, uneducated, too young, too old, to too scary? Or maybe it is the reverse: they won't accept me because I am female, male, fat, thin, poor, rich, black, white, handicapped, uneducated, etc.? This is an important side of this question because feeling inferior to others, ironically, is a virulent form of pride and responsible for much pain in the world.

The same judgments you pass on others are passed on you. By you. We need to humble ourselves before the Lord and acknowledge God's love for all of creation and so all people, including ourselves. We need to pray for God to show that love through us as we work with others.

The third question has to do with worry. Do you worry excessively about paying bills, earning an income, taking care of your family, etc., etc. etc....? I confess my answer to this question is usually, "Yes."

A story I came across recently has helped me gain a different perspective on this question. Have you ever seen those car seats for toddler-age children that include a steering wheel? The child looks so serious, as if what they are doing was really steering the car? And there sits Mom or Dad, the real drivers of the car, steering the vehicle with gentle amusement at their little one's efforts.

As I listened to this story, I realized I am like this child. Constantly stressing over steering in the right direction and all the time not realizing I am not completely in control of my life's direction. There are forces out there that have tried to usurp control and only an all-knowing God can manage them.

I find I hide a great deal of pride in my ability to take care of myself. It has made my life very difficult in many ways, because I have difficulty asking for help. As a single woman, living alone, I frequently need help with things; most recently when I was undergoing treatment for cancer and was not cleared to drive.

I realize I need to stop worrying and let the Divine Driver Drive; let God be God, acting when I am led to act, asking for help when I needed it. Keeping my openness to the Spirit alive and well.

A fourth question: Do you find it hard to repent? Or do you justify yourself for every time you hurt or injure another? It is easy to do. I have caught myself doing this. A short fuse due to a difficult day that has left you tired and cranky. A history of abuse that has left you untrusting and frustrated. Passing on the hurt you have received from others.

What we are forgetting in our litany of excuses is: we have still hurt someone. We cannot avoid guilt for doing to others by blaming it on what has been done to us. We still need to apologize and make it right if we can.

It takes humility to do that.

Question number five is a corollary to number four: Do you find it difficult to forgive others? It takes a great deal of humility to ask for forgiveness. It takes even more humility to forgive others. The only way to do that is by praying for them.

I have been learning, recently, how to pray for my enemies. The best way to pray for another is to lift them up to Christ for His blessing. My immediate reaction to this is best described with: "Aaaahhhh!!!!" I don't want them to be blessed! I want them to hurt as bad as I do. I want them to know what they have done to me! To my family! To my friends!

Yet we are commanded to do just that in Matthew 5:43-45:

> *"You have heard that it was said, 'You shall love your neighbor and hate your enemy.' But I say to you, Love your enemies and pray for those who persecute you, so that you may be children of your Father in heaven; for he makes his sun rise on the evil and on the good, and sends rain on the righteous and on the unrighteous."*

Matthew is saying God blesses all equally. If we are to be the child of our Father in heaven, we are to do the same. The only way to do this is through humility.

Ouch.

These test questions on humility are important questions to ask ourselves on a regular basis.

How important?

So important that if we do not find humility on our own, God will find it for us! The Scriptures tell us this in an interesting story about Belshazzar, related in Daniel 5:17-21:

> *"Then Daniel answered in the presence of the king, "Let your gifts be for yourself, or give your rewards to someone else! Nevertheless I will read the writing to the king and let him know the interpretation. O king, the Most High God gave your father Nebuchadnezzar kingship, greatness, glory, and majesty. And because of the greatness that he gave him, all peoples, nations, and languages trembled and feared before him. He killed those he wanted to kill, kept alive those he wanted to keep alive, honored those he wanted to honor, and degraded those he wanted to degrade. But when his heart was lifted up and his spirit was hardened so that he acted proudly, he was deposed from his kingly throne, and his glory was stripped from him. He was driven from human society, and his mind was made like that of an animal. His dwelling was with the wild asses, he was fed grass*

> *like oxen, and his body was bathed with the dew of heaven, until he learned that the Most High God has sovereignty over the kingdom of mortals, and sets over it whomever he will."*

Believe me. You don't want God to find humility for you!

But that is not all. In Daniel 10:10-12, we learn God responds to those who approach Him humbly:

> *"But then a hand touched me and roused me to my hands and knees. He said to me, 'Daniel, greatly beloved, pay attention to the words that I am going to speak to you. Stand on your feet, for I have now been sent to you.' So while he was speaking this word to me, I stood up trembling.*
>
> *"He said to me, 'Do not fear, Daniel, for from the first day that you set your mind to gain understanding and to humble yourself before your God, your words have been heard, and I have come because of your words.'"*

In the end, perhaps the best definition of humility is knowing you have fallen short of God's call in your life, repenting, then getting up, and trying again.

While all of the questions are important, the focus of this book will be to address the last two: Do you find it easy to repent? Do you find it easy to forgive? These are the two sneakiest of the questions that address humility. They disguise themselves as righteousness as in I have the truth and you do not. I have the high ground here and you need to accept that and repent for not seeing my way on this.

There is also the disguise of victim as in "I am the victim of many bad things happening in my life so you should just overlook the fact that I was rude, stole from you or killed you or a member of your family, because I am the real victim here."

In the meantime, "Are you humble? Yes or No?"

## Exercises

- Ask God to guide you as you meditate on the questions raised in this chapter.
    - What does it mean to "not have a clear picture of how others see you?"
    - Do you judge yourself and others based on your own standard of normal?
    - Do you worry excessively about paying bills, earning an income, taking care of your family, etc., etc. etc….?
    - Do you find it hard to repent? Or do you justify yourself for every time you hurt or injure another?
    - Do you find it difficult to forgive others? Or do you justify that as well?
- Practice the Consciousness Examen for each of the questions in this chapter, using one per day to give each of them full attention. Pray over each, one at time, asking God to bring to your attention the true answer of each for you. Write down any actions you feel led to take.
- Are you humble? Yes or No? Evaluate what each choice means to you based on the questions you have just asked yourself.

# The Sensation of God's Love

*"Love is patient; love is kind; love is not envious or boastful or arrogant or rude. It does not insist on its own way; it is not irritable or resentful; it does not rejoice in wrongdoing, but rejoices in the truth. It bears all things, believes all things, hopes all things, endures all things.*

*"Love never ends. But as for prophecies, they will come to an end; as for tongues, they will cease; as for knowledge, it will come to an end. For we know only in part, and we prophesy only in part; but when the complete comes, the partial will come to an end. When I was a child, I spoke like a child, I thought like a child, I reasoned like a child; when I became an adult, I put an end to childish ways. For now we see in a mirror, dimly, but then we will see face to face. Now I know only in part; then I will know fully, even as I have been fully known. And now faith, hope, and love abide, these three; and the greatest of these is love." I Corinthians 13:4-13*

Approximately six months after I was born, I nearly died of pneumonia. The story I was told went like this:

I was in the hospital and the elders from the church came to pray for me. They told my parents they were going to a prayer service held by the youth group my parents worked with. After the service, they would return to sit with them. While they were there, the doctor came in, checked me over, and told my parents if there was no change soon, I would not live until morning.

When the elders returned an hour later, I was well.

Forty-five years later, I was a devout Christian, the only one in my family to be so active in the church at that time. I was, myself, a self-sustaining elder in the church and had just applied for a full-time position. During the interview, I was asked one question for which I had no answer. "Your generation is essentially unchurched. Those that have continued in active church service have families who are active in church service. Yours is not. What has happened in your life to make you so active in the church?" I didn't have an answer. In fact, I had never thought about it before.

So, I prayed for awareness: "Why am I so active in the church when nobody else in my family is and my generation is so inactive?" Then I settled myself down into a meditation, and listened.

What came, blew me away!

I was, suddenly, laying in a crib in a darkened space. I looked towards the one light in the room and sitting there were my parents, but not as they are now. They looked like they did in my baby pictures.

It is hard to describe. Part of me didn't understand what was happening and had no words for it. I was overwhelmed by pain in my back and I couldn't get my breath. I was so hot and uncomfortable. I just hurt. The observer part of me understood I was running a fever and the painful shortness of breath was caused by pneumonia.

Then, I noticed a light coming from behind me, near the top of the crib. I realized it had been there for a little while, but I had only just noticed it because it was growing brighter than the light by my parents. I turned my head to look towards the light. Even though it was very bright now, I was not dazzled by it. I looked towards my parents, but they did not seem to react to the light.

When I looked back at the light, it was huge and beautiful; iridescent like a pearl and contained a presence I could not yet see. I felt no fear, only curiosity. At that point, a face emerged from the center of the light as if someone had just stepped from behind a curtain. She smiled at me. She: I call her "she", not because I saw a female shape for I only saw her face. I call her "she" because there was a definite sense of the feminine about this being, I would even say an archetypal feminine power emanated from the light. I have felt shadows of this power in some women I have met, but never containing the power this being conveyed. I felt no fear. Her presence was so filled with love and gentleness, only those holding on to their darkness could be afraid of her. Certainly, a baby could not fear this presence.

A hand-like projection of light came towards me, though I saw no hand. The light rested on my head like a gentle hand caressing my hair. As it did so, the light that composed it, slid down into me like a gentle, cool draught of water, but with the consistency of a light oil. I felt the observer of my older self speak softly the word "Love" and grow still.

The light continued to flow through me. Everywhere it touched me, the pain left and the darkness that caused the pain withdrew leaving more room for the light. I felt my chest ease and expand as it became easier to breath. My muscles that had been tensed against the pain and struggling with the effort to breathe began to relax. I felt a cooling sensation, relieving the uncomfortable heat of just minutes before.

When I was completely filled up with light and all the darkness and pain was gone, the "hand" withdrew. The loving face was smiling at me as it withdrew into the light. The light faded away to the darkness of the room.

I turned over to look for the light, then sat up. My parents hurried to my side.

A quiet voice whispered in my heart: "That is why you are still with the church. You have felt the sensation of love in this place."

I came to realize it was the sensation of love that healed me.

Why is this vision shared here?

Because it is that same sensation of love that brings us to the place of forgiving the unforgivable. It is this same sensation of love that allows us to release the pride that stands between us and repentance. It is the only force in the universe that can bring reconciliation.

When you read the scripture at the beginning of this chapter, you begin to realize love is something bigger than we have been living in this world. I have not found in this world anything even close to the love I experienced that night. The closest I have come is in most but certainly not all of the temples, mosques, sanctuaries, and natural sanctuaries of this earth...places that have been touched by God's presence.

I am active in my church because of that haunting spirit of love, hovering in the corners of these places. Some of these places no longer reflect this love because it has been driven out by the animosity, judgment, and pride of the people who now inhabit these once sacred spaces. This is true even between churches of the same denomination.

I don't stay in places like that.

The point is, you cannot truly forgive or repent without having some fragment of this love living inside you. To get this love inside you requires patiently spending time in the presence of God, letting God come into your heart and dwell there.

Practice the Presence!

Let's first look at the price of unforgiveness for it does have a price.

**Exercises**

- Practice Lectio Divina on I Corinthians 13:4-13 at the beginning of this chapter.

- Think of a time in your life when you experienced the sensation of accepting Love. Sit in silent meditation about the qualities of that Love. If you cannot think of a time when you had such an experience, pray for such an experience. Then sit in quiet meditation, expecting an answer. It may come when you least expect it, but it will come.

- Using I Corinthians 13:4-13, make some notes on how possessing the qualities listed would help you in the process of forgiving, repenting, and reconciling. Meditate on these qualities.

- Establish a practice of Consciousness Examen to assist you in recognizing and remembering these qualities as well as the sensation of love when you experience it.

# The Price of Unforgiveness

*"For if you forgive others their trespasses, your heavenly Father will also forgive you; but if you do not forgive others, neither will your Father forgive your trespasses." Matthew 6:14-15*

Once upon a time, there was a boy. Not a perfect boy, but he had a kind heart and a cheerful spirit. He liked people. And people liked him. He had many friends.

One evening, just before the Christmas after he graduated from high school, he went to a Christmas party at the restaurant where he worked. He gave rides to three boys who worked there also.

They never came home.

It took us four days to find the car with the four boys still inside. It was another week for the funeral, and months before the lawsuits were settled. It was a year before the full force of the cumulative sense of loss and anger that an insensitive media can do to a family when their is a sudden death of a loved one.

I started eating too much. I began spending too much. I couldn't sleep at night, and when I did sleep, I would be awakened by nightmares. I began having anxiety attacks. I developed a hair-trigger temper. And I began to be sick more and more often, missing more and more work.

Seeing a therapist helped somewhat. He told me I was angry.

I had not connected any of these symptoms to anger. Once I did, the nightmares and anxiety attacks stopped. I did not take the therapist's advice to write to the people who had made me so angry since, at the time, the lawsuits were not yet settled. It never occurred to me I didn't have to mail the letters.

So, the anger did not go away. It became stronger because I stuffed it inside. I justified my anger by the world's standards, but it was destroying my life. All I had to do was think about my brother, and I would be enraged. I would hate the whole world.

Then, one August evening almost two years after the accident, I was reading the Scriptures. By then, I was practicing my daily scripture study and prayer times more from habit than interest. I was terribly angry at God and had been feeling my prayers smack against the ceiling for some time. I was not paying close attention to what I was reading until I came across these words in Matthew 6:14-15:

> *"For if you forgive others their trespasses, your heavenly Father will also forgive you; but if you do not forgive others, neither will your Father forgive your trespasses."*

That stopped me cold. Instantly, I was furious! I yelled at God, "That's not fair! He was a good kid. These people hurt us and judged him unfairly. They made him the scapegoat."

Just then, I recalled another scripture passage:

> *"But I say to you, love your enemies and pray for those who persecute you,"* Matthew 5:44

"No! I can't do that! It hurts too bad! I hate them! After everything they did, I have a RIGHT to hate them!"

Suddenly, for the first time in my life, I felt truly alone. It was as if everything around me had frozen and was leaning forward, holding its collective breath. Although I lived on a busy street and had my windows open, there was suddenly no noise at all.

No car sounds. No bird sounds. Not even crickets. All was silent as if waiting for something.

Then came one sentence, firmly and sternly into my mind:

> "What RIGHT have you to hate someone I have chosen to love?"

Silence. Waiting. Then it came again, gently, more loving:

> "What right have you to hate someone I have chosen to love?"

Then, just as suddenly as they had gone, all the car sounds, bird noises, and cricket chirps came back. At last, I understood what was happening to me, what was really going on.

I was right. I did have some rights in all of this, but I understood it all wrong. God gave me the right to choose to follow God or not. When I chose to follow God, I gave up the right to hate anyone for any reason. If I did not choose God, all I had left was hate.

But then, I had already chosen God and sincerely committed myself as a disciple through baptism and confirmation many years before.

I prayed, "God, why is it so important to forgive? I don't understand, and it's so hard to do, and it hurts so badly. Please help me understand. Please help me obey because I cannot find it in me to even want to forgive."

I thought of a book I had read a couple of years before: C.S. Lewis's <u>The Great Divorce</u>. In this book, Lewis gives an imaginary glimpse of the entrance to heaven from the perspective of a visiting ghost from a gray world which existed in perpetual twilight. In one scene, a fellow visitor, a woman, is met by a man who hurt her badly many years before. He tries to explain to her how much he'd changed since they had known each other. How he had repented his actions. He knew how badly he had hurt her, and the man he now was would never have done such a thing. He asked her for forgiveness.

She could not give it. Not only that, she decided any place that would accept this man must not be heaven. A good God would never have forgiven such a man. The beauty of the place was an illusion and he was trying to trick her into staying. She was positive there would only be fire and brimstone beyond the beautiful mountains. She returned to the gray world; her hate was intact; yet unable to find heaven.

It suddenly occurred to me: if I had met any of the people I was angry with in heaven, would I have forgiven them? I did not like the answer to that question at all! All I could say was, "Oh, Lord, help me!"

It took two years of working at understanding forgiveness, before I was able to write a letter of peace to those people. It has taken many years and much practice in forgiving to completely release the anger of that year.

I have come a long way since then, but I have discovered something else I can do: I can think about my brother and remember the good times without anger. I could write the following poem in his memory after visiting his grave one Memorial Day:

### Timeless

Flowers color their spring across cold stone
as holly leaves drip their brown around
red berries crimped with age and weather
(a Christmas gift, not forgotten,
only disremembered.)

The stone chants its facts hard and cold
While young grasses play over a very young grave.

Memories flit over a mind numb
as a feeling like fear grips the heart,
invades the mind
taking it captive into a void of loneliness.

The shafts of many fingers slice red hot
through the chest and mind,
reaching for vital heart,
memory;
clutching, pulling, tearing,
until tears are wrung from the mind
as it watches dry-eyed in terror.

## Immortality Ltd.

An icy blast freezes the tears as numbness
creeps through darkness
pulling life and its meaning with it.
One grasps for it in panic
as one drowning, for a life preserver -
and catches –

And Catches -
Through the darkness -
Solid ground that brings

The soft spring of flowers color the young grasses
as they play across sun-warmed stone,
While, echoing from beyond time,
Comes the rasp of a rock
falling back from an empty grave.

## Exercises

- Follow the instructions for the Consciousness Examen, use one of the following statements or questions as your focus. Take the time to make notes on what you learned, and how you felt about the session. Schedule a time to act on anything you realized you needed to handle. What challenged you? What relieved you?
    - Show me what is holding back my relationship with God.
    - What offenses am I holding close that are causing me pain?
    - Show me what the root of my anger is.
    - Show me this day which has just passed and the thing(s) I need to remember about it.
- Follow the instructions for Lectio Divina, using one of the scriptures from this lesson. Make notes on anything you may have learned in this chapter. Did anything challenge you? Were there any surprises?

# The Deal Breaker

*"but whoever blasphemes against the Holy Spirit can never have forgiveness, but is guilty of an eternal sin—" Mark 3:29*

At the time I am writing this, it has been over 30 years since my brother died, and I am still learning about forgiveness and how essential it is to our spiritual growth and, interestingly, to our salvation. In fact, I've come to believe unforgiveness is the sin against the Holy Spirit spoken of in the Scriptures.

> *"Therefore I tell you, people will be forgiven for every sin and blasphemy, but blasphemy against the Spirit will not be forgiven." Matthew 12:31*

Before we go on, I want you to notice an important point from the autobiographical story told in the last chapter: I had developed a daily habit of prayer and scripture reading, maintained even when I didn't feel it was productive. I cannot emphasize the importance of daily, even twice daily prayer times. The more time spent with Jesus, the more you will become like him; the harder it will be to indulge in the luxury of anger and hatred. Look to the prayer forms in Appendix B for examples of the variety of functional methods of prayer available to you.

In 2 Corinthians 7:9-10, the Apostle Paul says,

> *"Now I rejoice, not because you were grieved, but because your grief led to repentance; for you felt a godly grief, so that you were not harmed in any way by us. For godly grief produces a repentance that leads to salvation and brings no regret, but worldly grief produces death."*

Then in Ephesians 4:30-32 we read:

> *"And do not grieve the Holy Spirit of God, with which you were marked with a seal for the day of redemption. Put away from you all bitterness and wrath and anger and wrangling and slander, together with all malice, and be kind to one another, tenderhearted, forgiving one another, as God in Christ has forgiven you."*

From these scriptures, we find repentance and forgiveness are of equal importance to God. There can be no reconciliation without both acts coming together. Constant daily prayer creates in us a godly grief which gives birth to both repentance and forgiveness. When we receive this godly grief, and give birth to repentance and forgiveness, the eternal sin of blasphemy against the Holy Spirit will be lifted from us. It is only an eternal sin when we hold on to the offense as a right and refuse to let it go.

This does not mean we are not allowed to be angry. Jesus was angry. Jesus' disciples were angry. God gets angry. What it means is we must move on from that anger. We must pray about it. We must find its roots and cut them out. We must raise our anger to God for guidance, movement forward, and release. In Ephesians 4:25-27 we read:

> *"So then, putting away falsehood, let all of us speak the truth to our neighbors, for we are members of one another. Be angry but do not sin; do not let the sun go down on your anger, and do not make room for the devil."*

We find the consummate scripture passage of the effects of unforgiveness and unrepentance on salvation in Matthew 18:21-38, The Parable of the Unforgiving Servant. This parable begins with Peter trying to figure out if there is a ceiling on how many times we need to forgive someone. He probably thinks as we are thinking, "There has to be a point when someone becomes unforgiveable. Surely, seven times is too many offenses to forgive!"

However, Jesus responds with a number that would be so difficult to track that it becomes infinite, "Not seven times, but, I tell you, seventy-seven times." (Matthew 18:22) If we are able to track seventy-seven offenses, we have not truly forgiven any of them. Then, to reinforce the lesson, Jesus does what he always did when teaching an important lesson. He told a parable:

> 'For this reason the kingdom of heaven may be compared to a king who wished to settle accounts with his slaves. When he began the reckoning, one who owed him ten thousand talents was brought to him; and, as he could not pay, his lord ordered him to be sold, together with his wife and children and all his possessions, and payment to be made. So the slave fell on his knees before him, saying, 'Have patience with me, and I will pay you everything.' And out of pity for him, the lord of that slave released him and forgave him the debt.
>
> "But that same slave, as he went out, came upon one of his fellow slaves who owed him a hundred denarii; and seizing him by the throat, he said, 'Pay what you owe.' Then his fellow slave fell down and pleaded with him, 'Have patience with me, and I will pay you.' But he refused; then he went and threw him into prison until he would pay the debt.
>
> "When his fellow slaves saw what had happened, they were greatly distressed, and they went and reported to their lord all that had taken place. Then his lord summoned him and said to him, 'You wicked slave! I forgave you all that debt because you pleaded with me. Should you not have had

> *mercy on your fellow slave, as I had mercy on you?' And in anger his lord handed him over to be tortured until he would pay his entire debt. So my heavenly Father will also do to every one of you, if you do not forgive your brother or sister from your heart."*

Let's look closer at this scripture passage so we might understand what it teaches us about forgiveness.

One talent is worth over 15 years wages to an average worker. This means the king had forgiven the first man 150,000 years' worth of wages. One denarius is worth one day's wage to an average worker.[1] This means the man who was forgiven 150,000 years' worth of wages refused to forgive 100 day's wages to his fellow worker. When the king heard of this lack of compassion, especially considering the depth of compassion the king had first shown to the unforgiving man, the king responded in anger, withdrew the blessing he had bestowed on the first man, and exacted every penny from him.

In this scripture passage, Jesus is saying each of us has been forgiven at least 150,000 years' worth of sins; sins we may not even know about or remember committing. In comparison, the hurt we receive from our neighbors is comparable to our sins against God as 100 days compares to 150,000 years.

God acts in the same way. If we do not forgive, we will not be forgiven. Even more frightening, whatever forgiveness we have received will be withdrawn.

Obviously, unforgiveness and unrepentance are deal-breakers for God. If we hold on to our anger and do not forgive; if we do not show the same mercy we are shown, we will end up needing to repent as much as we need to forgive. It is easy to see why this is true when we examine the Cycle of Unforgiveness in the next chapter.

The sin and blasphemy against the Holy Spirit has to be unforgiveness and unrepentance. It follows if only one thing will not be forgiven, and unforgiveness and unrepentance will not be forgiven, then this is the sin against the Holy Spirit.

---

[1] BibleGateway footnotes: https://www.biblegateway.com/passage/?search=Matthew+18%3A21-35&version=NRSV

But God sets boundaries on Himself as well as on us. Although the scriptures tell us in Matthew 6:14-15:

> *"For if you forgive others their trespasses, your heavenly Father will also forgive you; but if you do not forgive others, neither will your Father forgive your trespasses."*

I believe God does forgive us. God requires forgiveness from Himself just as He requires we forgive and for the same reasons. If we have already forgiven, it is easier to accept the repentance of others. This is why God can forgive us so easily when we do repent and turn away from our sins. He has already done the work of forgiving.

So, why do the scriptures say God will not forgive us? In 1 Corinthians 13:8-13, we discover how this will work:

> *"Love never ends. But as for prophecies, they will come to an end; as for tongues, they will cease; as for knowledge, it will come to an end. For we know only in part, and we prophesy only in part; but when the complete comes, the partial will come to an end. When I was a child, I spoke like a child, I thought like a child, I reasoned like a child; when I became an adult, I put an end to childish ways. For now we see in a mirror, dimly, but then we will see face to face. Now I know only in part; then I will know fully, even as I have been fully known. And now faith, hope, and love abide, these three; and the greatest of these is love."*

God is love. God will not allow anything inside of Himself that is not loving. Unforgiveness is not loving. What we are reading here is the answer to what constitutes "judgment" in God's eyes. The day will come when we will know all things about ourselves in the same way God knows them. We will see the truth behind our transgressions without excuses. We will know for ourselves how we could have avoided them and chose to transgress anyway. We will see for ourselves the backstory of what led to the offense against us, maybe even how it was never about us. We will even know the sorrow of the repentant heart we refused to forgive. Worse, we will know how petty that offense against us was in comparison to the offenses we, ourselves committed against God. Today, we only know the part we can see. In the "judgment", we will know the whole story. Unless we have built a foundation of forgiveness and repentance into our lives, we will be in despair. The thought we can be forgiven for all of this darkness residing in our hearts will never cross our minds. Like misbehaving children hiding from their parent, we will try to hide from God. So, locked in despair in our own guilt, we will achieve a level of depression unfathomable in this world.

Depression is a state of deep despair that renders the sufferer immobile and closed off from the rest of the world. Depressed people do not see the world as others see it, but see themselves as worthless, burdens on those who love them, and worthy of death. Depressed people can believe this so completely, they will come to believe it is better for their loved ones if they are dead and so many commit suicide. They cannot hear or feel the love and caring of others. If they do sense it, they see themselves as unworthy of such affection. They see themselves as forcing their loved one to waste their lives on something as worthless as the depressed person. It is not true but seems true to the depressed individual. The dark mirror is between them and the world.

This is how it will be in the "judgment". We will be judging ourselves. Trying to hide from God in our pain and despair, we flee from God into darkness, closing ourselves off from the loving presence; trying to commit spiritual suicide. That is not possible. We are eternal souls, and the darkness and suffering will never end.

We must develop the habit of forgiveness and repentance as early as we can to escape this. If we believe anything can be forgiven, we will know it in the face of this judgment. We will know we have a loving God who forgives all. We will know our sincere repentance will be met with loving forgiveness.

The best way to come to understand the difference between what we have been forgiven vs. what we need to forgive in others is to meditate on the body of Christ during Communion or Eucharist. Consider the following scripture passage:

> *"While they were eating, Jesus took a loaf of bread, and after blessing it he broke it, gave it to the*

> *disciples, and said, "Take, eat; this is my body." Then he took a cup, and after giving thanks he gave it to them, saying, "Drink from it, all of you; for this is my blood of the covenant, which is poured out for many for the forgiveness of sins. I tell you, I will never again drink of this fruit of the vine until that day when I drink it new with you in my Father's kingdom." Matthew 26:26-29*

Now, using one of the prayer forms from Appendix B, review this scripture carefully. I discovered through the Prayer of Imagination how petty my excuses for not forgiving seemed in the light of the forgiveness of Christ. For instance, when I looked at the petty lies of a co-worker which robbed me of a promotion and, eventually, my job, then compared it to Christ's forgiveness, I felt like a child refusing to forgive a playmate for eating my candy. For the first time, I saw the offense as God saw it, a childish bickering, and I was able to let the offense go. In other words, each communion, you come before the judgment seat of God, lay your life before the throne and repent. Then go forth whole and forgiven.

Communion is an ideal time to practice repentance and forgiveness if you wish for your participation in the sacrament to be deeper and more acceptable to God. Further, if you are donating to the church or any worthy cause, it is vital you are practicing forgiveness and repentance as seen in the following scripture:

> *"So when you are offering your gift at the altar, if you remember that your brother or sister has something against you, leave your gift there before the altar and go; first be reconciled to your brother or sister, and then come and offer your gift." Matthew 5:23-24*

If you hold anything against anyone or if they are holding anything against you, it is important to relieve this situation as much and as soon as possible. Your efforts will be blessed by God and your gift will be accepted.

**Exercises**

Take the passage from Matthew 18:21-38, The Parable of the Unforgiving Servant, as your text for the following exercises.

- Read the scripture from Matthew using Lectio Divina. Note any new insights that arise and how they apply to you.
- Read through the scripture in Matthew several times until you can remember all of its key points. Now meditate on it using the Prayer of Imagination. When you have finished the visualization, meditate on it and write down answers to the following questions:
    - What role did you play in the scene? (yourself as spectator, one of the crowd, the master, the forgiven slave, the victimized slave, etc.)
    - How was this role perfect for what you needed to learn from the scripture?
    - List the new insights you had on this scripture. How does this change or reinforce your understanding?

# The Cycle of Unforgiveness

*"You have heard that it was said to those of ancient times, 'You shall not murder'; and 'whoever murders shall be liable to judgment.' But I say to you that if you are angry with a brother or sister, you will be liable to judgment; and if you insult a brother or sister, you will be liable to the council; and if you say, 'You fool,' you will be liable to the hell of fire. So when you are offering your gift at the altar, if you remember that your brother or sister has something against you, leave your gift there before the altar and go; first be reconciled to your brother or sister, and then come and offer your gift. Come to terms quickly with your accuser while you are on the way to court with him, or your accuser may hand you over to the judge, and the judge to the guard, and you will be thrown into prison." Matthew 5:21-26*

This scripture in Matthew 5 speaks to us of reconciliation. We are to keep a close watch on ourselves for unresolved anger that shall open us up to judgment. Even insults and name-calling could bring us under condemnation if we are not careful. Consequently, when we are coming before God to present our gifts, we should examine ourselves carefully for anything we might have done to another for which we should make amends. If we find such a problem and have done nothing to set it right, we need to leave right then and work it out with them. Not to do so will make the offering of our lives during the communion unacceptable before God.

What Matthew 5:21-26 does is teach us the importance of paying attention to our thoughts and feelings regarding an offense. Developing such a habit prevents us from embarking on the Cycle of Unforgiveness.

Unforgiveness follows a cycle, circling in upon itself from the pinpoint of the offending act and, like a tornado, spreading out in an escalating spiral of anger, unforgiveness, and unrepentance. Unforgiveness is a black hole. The gravity of unforgiveness seeks to draw everyone around it into its vortex of hatred whether they want to be there or not. Everything is seen through the dark glasses of this hatred. Eventually, our entire lives become colored with suspicion, judgment, and hatred: you are for me or against me.

Let's look at how this spiral works.

First, something happens that we judge as inappropriate, ranging from merely being rude to horrendously criminal. Judging, in itself, is problematic. We are commanded by Christ not to judge. In Luke 6:37 we find:

> *"Do not judge, and you will not be judged; do not condemn, and you will not be condemned. Forgive, and you will be forgiven..."*

When people are confronted with this scripture, the reply is generally the passage from John 7:24:

> *"Do not judge by appearances, but judge with right judgment."*

I have met people who are sure they can "judge with right judgment".

But can we? Do we know all the factors in a person's life that led to the moment of offense? Are we aware of every nuance of a person's life that brings them to commit the act for which they are being judged? Do we know the intents of the offending party? Do we know the path of events leading to the resulting offense we see? Are we aware of the role we might have played in triggering the event?

No. Only God has all of this information. Only God knows all that led up to this moment when right became so wrong. Only God knows the environmental, cultural, societal, physical, mental, and emotional states that played a role in the act we feel we can rightly judge. Whether or not the perpetrator is using these states as an excuse for his or her behavior or is truly a victim of her or his circumstances. In the end, we are judging by appearances.

The result of our negative judgment is anger, the next step in the Cycle of Unforgiveness. We may say to ourselves, "How rude!" or "I'm having a terrible day and now this!" or "If I've told him or her once, I've told her or him a thousand times." Or perhaps it is a response to something horrific and life-changing; ranging from rape to racism; homicide to genocide. Our anger is raised. Our righteous indignation is brought forth. We begin to feel (as I did about my brother) we have a right to hate.

So our anger transforms into the next part of the spiral, hate. Hatred is a cancer of the soul. It creeps up on us without our knowing it's there. It undermines our health by creating damaging stress. It injures our ability to judge rightly because it shades our perception of events around us. Discrimination, sexism, homophobia, genocide, homicide, and rape, when closely examined, are all the results of festering anger turned into hatred. Hate is a complicated emotion, many times containing an element of fear. We tend to fear the things we hate because we develop expectations of harm from the object of our hatred. Hatred contaminates our other relationships, causing division when we perceive others as "taking sides" against us because they do not join us in our hate. Our entire way of seeing the world is deformed by our hatred. We begin to blame even the innocent for who they are. We become what we hate!

If we do not release our hatred with forgiveness, it becomes a block to love. It will eventually spill over into all of our relationships. People who are filled with hate cannot be filled with the spirit of love. Essentially, they are blocking God's efforts to influence their lives for good. 1 John 3:9-11 says:

## The Unforgivable Sin

> *"Those who have been born of God do not sin, because God's seed abides in them; they cannot sin, because they have been born of God. The children of God and the children of the devil are revealed in this way: all who do not do what is right are not from God, nor are those who do not love their brothers and sisters. For this is the message you have heard from the beginning, that we should love one another."*

We are commanded to love everyone, or we are not the children of God. Only the children of hate.

When we do not displace our hatred with forgiveness, we are replacing our relationship to God with something very dark. We take satisfaction in the misfortunes of our brothers and sisters while blaming them in some way for our misfortunes. I have sat with angry people who blamed other people for their sufferings, even when the other people could have in no way been responsible for the problem—blaming them for everything from cancer to traffic accidents. Blame is a disempowering belief, making the hate-filled person a victim with no control over what happens to them.

Then the cycle starts again:

*Judgement → Anger → Hate → Judgement → Anger → Hate*

Each turn makes us worse; we are dragged further and further from our relationship with God.

This cycle destroys all relationships—with our family, with our friends, with our bosses and coworkers, even with strangers because it demands all who would affiliate with us to hate what and whom we hate. We are alienated from, even attack those who do not hate what or whom we hate, but the truly serious result of unforgiveness is alienation from God. Alienation from God is the real price of sin.

One of the best examples I have seen of this cycle in action was at a week-long retreat I attended a number of years ago. Two women were sharing a room across the hall from mine. I could get the gist of everything they said to each other because one of them had a strong voice that carried down the hallway. They were obviously the best of friends and had been since they were children. The louder one was obviously possessed by anger and hatred toward an ex-husband from whom she had been divorced for several years. Her friend was single.

One afternoon, while returning to my room after lunch, I knew something was very wrong. I could hear the divorced woman screaming at her friend even before I entered the hallway. From what she was saying, I realized her single friend had just told the divorced woman she was dating her ex-husband.

It was obviously the worst betrayal of trust the divorced woman had ever experienced. She ranted on and on for an hour as she packed to move out of the room. Some of the things she said over and over again, "How could you!? Haven't you been listening to me?! I thought we were on the same wavelength here! Why have you gone behind by back and done such a terrible thing to me?!" Well, you get the picture.

The divorced woman moved out to another room and, from what I can tell, didn't speak to her old friend for the rest of the retreat. Her unforgiving anger toward her ex-husband had now cost her a best friend.

This cycle is the source of the proliferation of hate in our world and at the heart of every dispute and war. It disguises and excuses itself as pride, loyalty, patriotism, righteousness, justice, and even love. In reality, unforgiveness is the opposite of all of these things. It does not serve your self-esteem to stand on your pride in conflict situations. It only makes you look small. It does not show loyalty to your friends or organizations to refuse to associate with those who do not share your anger or hatred. It closes your mind to the God-given gifts of those who can improve your world. It is not serving your country to hate its enemies but endangers it by destroying its peace, killing its youth, and undermining its infrastructure through exorbitant expenditures on armaments.

If Jesus taught us anything, he taught us it is not in the service of God to judge your neighbor based on strangling dogma. He taught us if we are in service to our fellow human beings, we are only in service to our God. In the Parable of the Judgment of the Nations in Matthew 25:31-46. Jesus sets the example for us by giving to whoever asked of him without questioning religious or social affiliations. You cannot show love for another by hating who they hate. Hate contaminates love and creates distrust which moves like cancer into all of our other relationships.

We cycle into a lonely, loveless life.

## Exercises

- Think about a stituation you are having trouble forgiving. On a fresh sheet of drawing paper, draw a circle, incorporating the words from the Cycle of Unforgiveness into the rim of the circle. Now, using the Mandala meditation from the Using Artwork prayer, begin to fill in your circle.

- Look up Matthew 25:31-46. (A copy can be found in Appendix A) Study it using Lectio Divina or Visualization Practice. If you are feeling particularly brave, practice Consciousness Examen, asking the Spirit to show you where you fall under judgment in the light of this scripture.

- Practice the Lord's Prayer as laid out in Appendix B for a week. At the end of that time, notice any deepening in your relationship with God.

# Breaking the Cycle

*"I did then what I knew best, when I knew better, I did better."* Maya Angelou

*"Forgiveness is made easy when we can identify with others and admit to our own imperfections and an equal capacity for wrongdoing."* Leo Buscaglia

How do you break the Cycle of Unforgiveness? The cycle is simple to break, but not easy. Because the longer the cycle has been established, the harder it is to break. It becomes hard-wired into your neural pathways: a habit of thought. The best way to break the cycle is to become aware you are entering that endless loop before it starts—in the initial judgment stage.

When you find yourself judging someone and growing angry, catch yourself. Count to ten if you must, but catch yourself judging. If it helps, memorize the scripture passage about judging from Matthew 7:1-3:

> *"Do not judge, so that you may not be judged. For with the judgment you make you will be judged, and the measure you give will be the measure you get. Why do you see the speck in your neighbor's eye, but do not notice the log in your own eye?"*

Ask questions, either during prayer or with the input of a mentor or trusted friend whose opinion you know will be balanced and truthful:

- Remind yourself: Rarely is the rude behavior of another individual about you. Most of the time, a person is already in the unforgiveness cycle, and you just got in the way. Repeat to yourself, "It's not about me!"
- Why do I find this person's action offensive? Did they hurt my feelings? Frighten me? Surprise me? Or did they cross a personal boundary I established because I am in an unforgiveness cycle of my own?
- Am I angry because they violated my expectations of them? Of the organization they represent? Of my expectations of the results? Is this abnormal behavior from them and so startled me? Can I think of a reason for their response that may have nothing to do with me? Could there be such a reason?
- Is this a big enough deal in my life to waste time on anger? In another day/week/month/year, will it matter? Is it just an insult to my pride? Is my pride so fragile that this could damage it? If so, why am I so touchy?
- Is this behavior the reaction to a problem the person is worried about and I may be able to do something to help?
- In other words, is this offense worth risking my soul over?

By the time you come this far in your self-examination; you will usually have cooled off either because you have reminded yourself of a good reason for the behavior or just gave yourself space to cool down. If you are still battling judgmental thoughts, pray about the situation. Turn it over to God for further insights and understandings or just let it go.

When you treat all offenses this way, you will find yourself growing angry much less often, and your growth in understanding and fostering of relationships with other people will be amazing. It also can save you from lost friendships and embarrassing situations when you find out the real reason for the offending behavior of a friend has more to do with their pain than with you.

You might even find yourself developing the much sought after but rarely found "peace of Christ."

If you are already stuck in the Cycle of Unforgiveness, it is much more difficult to release your anger, especially if you have been working through the cycle for a long time. In these cases, I find I need help to let the offenses go. I begin a process I call the Cycle of Forgiveness.

## Exercises

- Set aside time for the Consciousness Examen each evening or morning for the next 30 days, making notes of what comes up. Let the theme of your meditations be to improve your ability to forgive and repent. While other things may come up, the specified theme will be brought more and more to your attention. At the end of the 30 days, review your notes to recognize how much closer you have grown to God.

- Pick an offense you are having trouble forgiving or repenting. Using the Walking Meditation, ask Jesus to bring to your mind all the issues involved as you go out on your walk and then help you release these issues as you return. If you would like, you can combine the Walking Meditation with Visualization Practice and imagine Jesus walking with you and counseling you.

- Create a Mandala from the Using Artwork Prayers while thinking of the person who has offended you. Sometimes an approach from outside the logical mind can bring you more insights than the logical mind can face.

# Cycle of Forgiveness

*"See that none of you repays evil for evil, but always seek to do good to one another and to all. Rejoice always, pray without ceasing, give thanks in all circumstances; for this is the will of God in Christ Jesus for you. Do not quench the Spirit. Do not despise the words of prophets, but test everything; hold fast to what is good; abstain from every form of evil." I Thessalonians 5:15-22*

I Thessalonians 5:15-22 tells us not to retaliate when evil is done to us. This is evident in the life of Christ. He does not call down fire on towns that refuse him entry; he does not curse the Roman soldiers who crucify him; he even rebukes his followers when they try to protect him from those who would arrest him. We need to keep Jesus' example in mind if we are to break the cycle of unforgiveness.

The first defense against the Cycle of Unforgiveness is to establish a habit of daily prayer and scripture study. As it did for me when I found Myself so angry following my brother's death, a daily spiritual practice leaves you open to God's influence and the movement of the Spirit in your life even when it does not feel like it is moving. Spiritual practices of scripture study, prayer, and especially expressing gratitude to God for your life and the world around you is the greatest safeguard you have against anger and hatred. If you have not established a daily habit of prayer and scripture study, now would be a good time to start. It is your first step in the Cycle of Forgiveness.

Rejoicing in Praise and Gratitude to God is the second step in the Cycle of Forgiveness because it is a great way to focus your attention away from the hurt and on to God. Why gratitude? We have this exhortation from Paul in the I Thessalonians scripture that opens this chapter. We will refer back to this scripture again in this section so you may want to keep track of it.

Rejoicing in Praise and Gratitude to God should be part of every prayer you pray. Sing it! Dance it! However you feel rejoicing, whether reading or writing a psalm or allowing it to spill over into bodily expression, this is an important part of prayer. If you cannot think of anything to praise or be grateful for, pray for this awareness. The longer you look for things to be grateful for, the more you will find.

The next habit to foster is a difficult, but simple one. When you find yourself becoming angry: Stop. Just stop. Count to ten. Take a walk. Do not spend the time plotting revenge, but do as I Thessalonians tells you and "test everything" about the situation. If you don't stop, you will be in danger of retaliating or "repaying evil for evil." If you have trouble controlling your temper and have a habit of allowing your anger to flash out without thinking about it first, a daily practice of Consciousness Examen will go a long ways in helping you control your anger. Not being able to control your temper is a juvenile reaction and has no place in the life of an adult. I know people who feel expressing their anger immediately and without examination of the situation is a strength and a sign of toughness. It is actually a sign of weakness and lack of self-control. Anger of this kind leaves you lonely and friendless as your family and friends get tired of walking on eggs around you and eventually fade out of your life.

The scriptures say the meek are to inherit the earth. There are many that scoff at this, seeing it as a sign of weakness, but let's explore what that word "meek" really means.

In the auto industry, there is a tool called a "meek hammer." It is several stories high and consists of a platform on which rests a mold of a car body. A sheet of metal is laid over the top and a large "hammer" with the other half of the mold is hoisted to the ceiling and dropped on the metal in order to mold an entire car body in one, swift motion. The hammer can be set to fall very precisely. So much so that a watch can be set on its base and the adjustment made so that the hammer stops just above the crystal without even scratching it. It is called "meek" because that is what it is: power in control.

The habit of spending of your power in anger is what makes this simple, new habit of "stopping" so incredibly difficult yet so vitally important. If you are not used to controlling yourself, your power may be great, but it will crush many delicate things such as your relationships with friends and family. Then they are gone from your life and you have nothing but your anger. It is a terrible and lonely place to live.

God will help you with this. The daily practice of the Consciousness Examen is an invaluable tool for breaking habits of anger.

The next habit to foster within your prayer life is to pray for God's perspective on any given situation, a further "test everything" process. If you are locked in a pattern of unforgiveness, praying specifically for God's perspective can open your mind to a larger point of view. Ask for an open mind to anything the Spirit may be bringing to your attention. Ask for recognition and help in accepting any role you may have played in the conflict. Ask for assistance in releasing your anger. Write up the many facets of the conflict as accurately as you can remember and present them to God for assistance in forgiving them. Ask for humility in the face of your anger.

Then, study the events surrounding the crucifixion and Jesus' words from the cross. If anyone had reason to be unforgiving, it was Jesus at that moment. Yet he forgave everyone who participated in his death. That includes those for whose sin he died, even you. A particularly profound moment for this type of meditation is in preparation for receiving the bread and wine in the sacrament of communion or Eucharist. This is a moment when the divine touches earth, when the earthly takes on the divine so we might be reminded of Whose we are. Perspective is obtained at such moments. Even, intervention.

The fifth step in this cycle and perhaps the most important of all: Pray for your enemy! Matthew 5:43-45 tells us:

> *"You have heard that it was said, 'You shall love your neighbor and hate your enemy.' But I say to you, Love your enemies and pray for those who persecute you, so that you may be children of your Father in heaven; for he makes his sun rise on the evil and on the good, and sends rain on the righteous and on the unrighteous."*

This command can be extremely difficult to obey. Sometimes, when I am angry, the best prayer I can muster is "God, help me to pray for this person." Praying for the person who has offended you is an important step in freeing yourself of your rage. When you can pray for your enemy, you will begin to heal. You begin to experience compassion and a softening of heart towards the other person. You will even be open to understanding the strains the other person was under when the offense was committed. That compassion is a gift given to you by God.

How do you pray for an enemy? While this was discussed earlier in this book, it is important enough to be brought to your attention again. We pray for our enemies by lifting them up to God in humility and love for a blessing. That may be a little much to ask when you are so angry you are imagining ways to harm them, but, until you can do this, you are still under condemnation. You are still sinning.

Fifth: act. Approach the offending person and share your hurt and apologize for any harm you have done in retaliation for the hurt. Depending on the type of offense, you may want to request mediation. Mediation is a way to create reconciliation. All parties in a dispute present their perception of the conflict and work with a professional mediator to resolve the issues involved. There are certified mediators who can help you. The International Mediation Institute is one resource for connecting with a mediator.

It may be the offense is a criminal act. The Holy Spirit will help you to understand whether or not the best thing to do is to take legal action against the offender or work with a mediator. Sometimes both may be called for. Hate crimes, robbery, and personal violations of many kind are illegal, and the offender can be prosecuted. Some offenses may not be illegal but have created a financial burden on the victim. You may feel the legal action of a lawsuit is in order. Pray about it first. Make sure legal action is not an act of revenge born out of anger or hate while you are locked in the Cycle of Unforgiveness.

Another useful tool is letter-writing as suggested by my therapist so many years ago. I have written many such letters since, but I have never mailed them. Writing a letter I know I will never mail frees me to write down everything I am feeling; getting all of those hard, dark feelings out in the open. Sometimes, you develop a new perspective of the situation. Sometimes, you even find the part you played to cause the situation.

The letters allow me to confront my judgments and the reasons behind them; many times they reveal a long-standing Cycle of Unforgiveness in myself I had not recognized until it was tapped by recent events. Letter-writing allows me to release that cycle and, in doing so, set myself free from it. Sometimes, it takes several letters as God leads me through the process of forgiving. If you journal regularly, this would be a good practice for you. However, do not use your journal to write the letter. It must be an actual letter you could mail if you needed to do so. It also allows you the release of destroying the letter when you are finished.

The last paragraph of the letter I write is always a prayer to God to take my feelings and set me free from them. I sign the letter. I let it sit overnight. The next day, I quietly sit as I would when I am preparing for prayer. Then I read the letter out loud, letting myself feel all the feelings of anger, hate, fear, and sadness. When I get to the prayer portion, I pray it with all my heart, sometimes on my knees. Then I destroy the letter in an act of release and forgiveness. If you are ready to let the offense go and do this practice in faith, believing God hears your prayer, the bad feelings go away with the letter.

One time, there came a point in my Cycle of Forgiveness when I was having extreme difficulty letting go of my anger against a couple of people. Not even the letters freed me from the burden of anger I carried towards them. I prayed about it in my journal. I asked, "Why is it nothing I do frees me of my anger towards these few people when I have been able to forgive others far worse things?"

God moved in my heart, and I realized these people had one thing in common: They were people I felt should have known better than to do what they did. They were all church people: Ministers; Christians I thought of as leaders in the church; friends I had known for many years, and yet they gossiped about and attacked me in ways that damaged my reputation and my career. I heard myself say to God, "How will these people ever learn to behave in a Christ-like manner if I don't teach them to do better?"

Then God showed me the lack of faith in my question. God reminded me of Philippians 1:6:

> *"I am confident of this, that the one who began a good work among you will bring it to completion by the day of Jesus Christ."*

It occurred to me if God is working a good work in me, then God is certainly working the same good work in those around me. It may be that I will be involved in that good work, but it is not my task to begin it on my own. My task is to forgive and have the faith to believe God is working with them as well as with me.

I was able, then, to release and forgive these last few people. As I did so, I realized all forgiveness and repentance are acts of faith. All unforgiveness and unrepentance are actions lacking in faith.

One last point. If you have been in the habit of hating for some time and your hatred has become hard-wired in your brain, you have developed a hating habit, even an addiction to hate. All habits and addictions are hard to break, but a thought habit is the hardest because your brain is always there, always thinking. The best, and frankly, the easiest way to free yourself of thought habits is the prayer practice of the Consciousness Examen. This prayer asks God to monitor you in order to free you from habits of thought and addiction.

> *"Then Jesus said to the Jews who had believed in him, "If you continue in my word, you are truly my disciples; and you will know the truth, and the truth will make you free." John 8: 31-32*

## Exercises

- On a fresh sheet of drawing paper, draw a circle, incorporating the words from the Cycle of Forgiveness into the rim of the circle. The key words for the circle are:
    - Good prayer and study habits
    - Gratitude
    - Perspective
    - Crucifixion
    - Pray for enemy
    - Mediate
    - Letter writing
    - Working a good work
    - Consciousness Examen

  Now, using the Mandala meditation from the Using Artwork prayer, begin to fill in your circle. This will also help you to review whether you have tried all of the available avenues for healing.

- Continue to set aside time for the Consciousness Examen each evening or morning for the next 30 days, making notes of what comes up. Let the theme of your meditations be to improve your ability to forgive and repent. While other things may come up, the specified theme will be brought more and more to your attention. At the end of the 30 days, review your notes to recognize how much you have grown closer to God.

# Principalities and Powers

*"For our struggle is not against enemies of blood and flesh, but against the rulers, against the authorities, against the cosmic powers of this present darkness, against the spiritual forces of evil in the heavenly places." Ephesians 6:12*

There came a time when I began to work on what I called "free-floating anger": Anger that was just there without being attached to any particular person or time or place. I could not nail down a source for this anger. I would become angry beyond what the situation called for, and I would become angry fast; in a flash.

When I came across the above scripture in Ephesians 6, I knew I was experiencing anger at my social condition—anger at the sexism, ageism, poverty, and even discrimination against single women in our society. When a person experiences this kind of anger without conscious awareness, they are a pressure cooker waiting to explode.

The conditions of your social environment are constantly dinging you. For example, a singles ministry leader calls the women he works with "Old Maids." Suddenly your suggestions must be checked out with the "younger" or "older" adults. You don't get or keep a job because you are male, female, black, Hispanic, gay, too young, or too old. You become highly sensitised to all discrimintory practices that fall within your realm of experience, and not just those directed towards yourself personally. You begin to see your particular brand of discrimination in any act of unfairness, even when it is not there.

One day someone does something discriminating, maybe outrageously so or maybe just rude, and BAM! you go off like dynamite. Maybe you don't even understand why this time is different when you were able to keep it together before, even under similar circumstances. In August of 2015 there is a racism backlash with the police in the United States that has resulted in a year of a violence people thought had ended in the 1960s. But it hasn't ended because the "dinging" hasn't ended. Fifty years of repeated discrimiatory acts, of both small and large encounters, has created a powder keg of anger that has finally exploded as it did in the 1950s and '60s.

How do you recognize this anger for what it is?

My wake-up call came when, one day, I realized my anger response was inappropriate to the circumstance that initiated it. That is, my response to the offending action was greater than the action that triggered it. I became aware of this during my regular prayer and meditation time.

Upon praying for guidance and meditating on my anger response, I realized I was approaching all people in this group with an expectation. I was expecting to be excluded, ridiculed, and left out in some way for who I am while, at the same time, hoping it wouldn't happen. Each time it happened as I expected instead of as I had hoped, my anger response was much worse. While I know that people in leadership roles are no different from other people in their social group, deep down I expect firemen, police officers, ministers, political leaders, etc. to set better examples of behavior than the regular members of the groups they represented.

Rage against discrimination is a rage born of helplessness—to face loss of job, loss of status, or loss of anything because of who you are, not what you did is a helpless feeling. It is made more painful because it undermines (and is meant to undermine, even if subconsciously) your self-respect, your self-confidence, and your ability to move on in a positive way.

Still, we are commanded to forgive such treatment.

Impossible, yet here we are! Daily, we are dinged for being female, male, black, Hispanic, single, divorced, widowed, too old, too young, too short, too tall, too fat, too thin, disabled, Christian, Jew, or Muslim. In short, for being ourselves, even being alive. The very fabric of our social environment is woven to exclude the very fabric from which we are made!

And we are to forgive it all but in a very, particular way.

This kind of anger is extremely difficult to release because discriminatory practices are widespread and constantly attacking you. I have prayed about it and received a very unsatisfying answer:

We are to forgive while standing for who we are.

However, this is a particular kind of standing. We stand as witnesses. We stand as Watchers. We stand as those who notice, not just what is happening, but the deep roots of what is happening.

No action is just what it seems on the surface. All actions are like dandelions. They have deep roots into our pasts, into the history of who we are with each other. If we are only addressing the current action, the little plant on the surface, plucking at only the little yellow flower of violence we see before us while ignoring the huge, deep roots sustaining and feeding it, the issues will never be resolved. The plant will spring back as if it had never been addressed, because it hasn't.

When we stand in this way, we are standing in obedience to God. When we stand in obedience to God, we begin to see things as God sees them, using God's anger which is grounded in love. And so, we are not only able to forgive this offensive behavior and mistreatment, but we are able to forgive it while it is happening. God's anger is an anger that hates the action but loves the person. Obedience to God opens us up to God's wisdom and insight in how to address the situations confronting us.

Consequently, this kind of anger is used in a very peculiar way.

This anger is an ironic gift given to the downtrodden and discriminated against, not to be used to build hate, but to reclaim society as a whole for God's Kingdom. Because marginalized people are so intimately attuned to the shortfall of the societies we live in, we are the ones who can point it out and work for change. We are the ones who can bring the kingdom closer. Further, we can use this process to develop humility in place of hate by making ourselves more aware of how our own actions, arising from these deep roots, harm others.

The way in which this anger must be used is as a catalyst for right action in the face of hatred. This anger is to give us the strength and courage to stand before those who would beat us down. We are to stand as Christ stood: enduring all without judgment and without bowing to the temptation to hate, heaping coals of forgiveness on the heads of our enemies, praying for them even as they beat us down. We are to stand while remembering that our persecutors are as much victims of their social condition as we are. ("Father, forgive them, for they do not know what they are doing." Luke 23:34) We are called to live in the way George Herbert, English minister and metaphysical poet, describes: "Living well is the best revenge."

Living well! We are to exercise all the faith, courage, and strength of who we are as children of God, facing the discrimination head on while going about our business in spite of profiling and illegal detention; while our education, gifts, and experience are ignored, belittled, or denied. We are to do it while not becoming like those who attack us. We are to do it without allowing ourselves to be brought down to their level.

When we do this, we rise to our better selves and show the haters who we are and in doing so, who they are. By being who we are created to be and turning the other cheek when victimized, we disprove the prejudice against us, rise above the discrimination heaped upon us, and allow God's judgment to flow without earning that judgment against ourselves. Our example becomes a testimony before God against our accusers.

We overcome by being our best selves.

And many will die doing it. Many will be raped, jailed unjustly, and beaten. Many will die with their great gifts from God unused, the societal cost of discrimination. Many will not have the courage, the strength, or the perseverance to stand. But it is only in standing that this negative social condition will be addressed and cleared away. It was only when Rosa Parks quietly continued to be her human self, tired and in need of rest in the face of discrimination that people finally registered what was happening in a real way, and the movement against such petty acts erupted around her. It was Gandhi's peaceful protests that finally led to India's release from British rule.

Another example of standing for who you are was the Million Man March on Washington, D.C. On August 27-28 1963, more than 200,000 people gathered in Front of the Lincoln Memorial on the National Mall, to march for jobs and freedom. Civil rights activists A. Philip Randolph and Bayard Ruskin organized the march. The National Association for the Advancement of Colored People and the Southern Christian Leadership Conference, who had to put aside their own differences to take part, both backed the march. President John F. Kennedy who was looking for support for the passage of the Civil Rights Act allowed the march to take place. While the hospitals were prepared for the violence they were sure would follow and the Pentagon had assembled 19,000 troops, there was no violence and not one arrest. Bayard Ruskin said, "We need, in every community, a group of angelic troublemakers."

Again, on January 22, 2017, the Women's March on Washington inspired approximately 2.3 million women from around the world to take a stand against misogynistic treatment espoused by new leadership in Washington. The protests were, once more, handled without violence or arrests in cities around the world.

The best current example of what it means to stand in the face of discrimination is President Barack Obama. His steady and courageous service to his country while ignoring the obvious racial antagonism of Congress only made their racist mindset more obvious, petty, and childish as they engaged in measures that can only be interpreted as a refusal to serve their country in their elected capacity.

But many will lower themselves to the expectations of those who classify them as less than human. Such actions only confirm the fears and feed the ignorance of their detractors.

On an international scale, unforgiveness and unrepentance stand beside greed as one of the root causes of war. Many groups are organized to respond to such actions with varying degrees of violence. The list is too long to write here, but all of these groups exist in response to the persecution they can no longer tolerate.

The people responding to these defensive measures, do not understand the protests and violence are a reaction to what they, themselves, have done. These people are blinded by their social environment. They never see the discrimination and persecution their culture has heaped upon the people their social mores have judged as less deserving than others, and so they see these groups' responses to the cultural violence of discrimination as coming out of nowhere. Their victims retaliate with groups of their own, and the violence escalates.

The church and the media, forces in existence to make us aware of such discriminating behaviors, have instead conspired with the social environment to blind its people to the violence of their actions and perpetuate its myth of superiority. The churches manipulate the gospel into an exclusive message it does not contain. The media is more interested in publishing the sensational, misleading statements, and selective "facts" that make a great story because they "sell". The media has traded courage and truth for financial gain, nearly destroying the country in the process.

We have war. We have arms proliferation. We have "decent citizens" killing other "decent citizens" because their free-floating anger has responded, not just to criminal activity, but to a misunderstanding, an error in judgment, or a simple mistake with pulling their concealed weapon and shooting without questions, without thinking, without even counting to ten. In one second, committing a sin for which no restitution is possible.

Because we do not forgive one another, the work of hatred and fear goes on.

We must foster in ourselves the courage to see past our social environment by confronting our congregations, our media, and our financial, cultural, and political environments with the love of Christ for all peoples. We must learn to see past our upbringing to that place of peace and justice. We must groom in ourselves the habit of thought to hear the words "unforgiveable," "hate," "judgment," and "Them vs. Us" as alarm bells—warning signals of discrimination and unforgiveness in ourselves. We must pray for the courage of faith to release our fear of the unknown and those that are culturally different from ourselves. If we do not, we are in danger of losing our relationship to God and destroying our world while instigating another holocaust.

We must learn to see one another as human beings, equally loved by God, and as such, brothers and sisters trying our best, some of us against incredible odds. Only in this way can fearful and hate-filled discriminating and segregating social environments be transformed.

Remember, the response you got is the message you sent.

**Exercises**

- Continue to set aside time for the Consciousness Examen each evening or morning for the next 30 days, making notes of what comes up. Let the theme of your meditations be to improve your ability to forgive and repent. While other things may come up, your requested theme will be brought more and more to your attention. At the end of the 30 days, review your notes to recognize how much you have grown closer to God.
- Using Consciousness Examen again, ask Jesus to bring to your mind an act of violence you may not have considered to be violence. Don't be surprised if you find yourself confronted with something you did that was discriminatory without you realizing it. Begin to pray about this situation, asking for more light and love to be pressed into this situation.

# Obstacles to Forgiveness

*"Then Peter came and said to him, 'Lord, if another member of the church sins against me, how often should I forgive? As many as seven times?' Jesus said to him, 'Not seven times, but, I tell you, seventy-seven times.' Matthew 18:21-22*

Obstacles to forgiveness are those things that prevent us from taking action, that keep us from engaging in the processes we need to free us from the burden of anger and sin. These are our defense mechanisms to shield us from the effects of those activities we view as damaging to our families or ourselves. Included as obstacles are:

- The inability to separate the offending action from our response to that action
- The inability to separate our response to the offending action from the repercussions to the offending individual
- Obsession with the circumstance
- The magnitude of the offense
- Denial of responsibility for our role in the offense
- Misunderstanding the role of forgiveness in the situation

- Self-preservation or protection, and
- Misunderstanding the meaning of reconciliation

Let's explore each of these obstacles separately.

*The inability to separate the offending action from our response to that action.* This obstacle concerns how we respond to the people around us. We fail to understand that our response is a choice we make, not a choice someone makes for us. We can hear our relinquishment of responsibility in comments such as this, "That made me so angry!" Nobody "makes" you angry. Anger is your chosen response to a circumstance, and you can choose to make a different response. Truthfully, the statement should read: "This happened, and I choose to be angry about it!" When we say something made us angry, we are accepting the role of victim. We are telling ourselves another person has power over us, and so we are unable to act for ourselves.

Such self-victimization takes away your power and makes you fearful. Fear is a huge contributor to anger. You are admitting you have lost control of your life and your life choices. Such a belief weakens your ability to make choices for your life. Such a belief robs you of your ability to forgive. Nobody makes you angry. You have chosen an anger response for yourself. When you realize this, you can now choose another response and free your life. The sooner you understand this, the easier your life will be and the easier it will be to forgive.

*The inability to separate our response to the offending action from the repercussions to the offending individual.* Many people, including myself as reported earlier, have mistakenly believed holding anger punishes the offending individual. That never happens. Anger destroys the person holding it, not the person towards whom it is directed. Anger is not a weapon. Anger is a vice. Like all vices, it destroys the possessor. It has no effect on the object of your anger.

Even worse, eventually, you begin to realize the object of your anger is not being harmed by your anger. When this happens, your anger will drive you to bring harm to that individual. You become like your enemy. You become the offender.

The only way to stop the escalation of violence is to strike at its center: the anger we self-righteously hold as a right. We forget the statements in Ephesians 4:25-27:

> *"So then, putting away falsehood, let all of us speak the truth to our neighbors, for we are members of one another. Be angry but do not sin; do not let the sun go down on your anger, and do not make room for the devil."*

When we keep our anger, we make room for sin. Our unforgiveness separates us from God. It destroys us, not the object of our anger.

*Obsession with the circumstance.* Something causes us fear, pain, or embarrassment. We rehearse it again and again in our minds: what they did; what we did; what they should have done; what we should have done; how we should have responded on and on ad infinitum. Our original response to the event may not have been all that angry at first, but we stew on it a little; we visit with family, friends and coworkers about the offense who respond angrily out of loyalty to us; and soon we have full-blown rage to deal with!

When we dwell on slights and offenses, they escalate into major traumas in our minds. They become blown out of all proportion to the offense. We often see this in our church families. Something happens between two people in the congregation and, before you know it, the whole congregation is split into angry factions with members leaving.

As we continue to relive, revisit, or review the offense, the worse it becomes in our minds until we can't let go of our anger. Churches divide over the color of the new carpet in the sanctuary, totally forgetting the first Christians had no sanctuary let alone carpet. The sooner you catch and release this obsessive reviewing of offenses, the sooner (and easier) it will be to forgive it.

*The magnitude of the offense.* Sometimes it is the nature of the offense that stops us from forgiving: genocide, war, any attack on a child, any attack on a loved one, hate crimes, racism, sexism. All of these (and many others besides) seem too terrible ever to be forgiven. In fact, merely mentioning the need to forgive such "crimes against humanity" may cause us to wonder about the sanity of the person making the suggestion. As Christians, the command to forgive still stands before us. It stands before us as a warning lest we become like those we hate.

We are not disloyal or unpatriotic by forgiving such things. Neither are we supporting the perpetrators by practicing forgiveness. Instead, by forgiving, we become free to deal with the issues behind such crimes. We are free to love and so take appropriate action to prevent such crimes from happening in the future. Instead of reinforcing the hatred of the perpetrator with callous indifference, we are able to make room to understand the perpetrator's position and what led to their damaging response. We are acting out of faith in God to confront these crimes in the best way possible. A prime example of this way of dealing with such heinous crimes is the Truth and Reconciliation Commission established by former South Africa President Nelson Mandela to provide restorative justice for victims of apartheid.

*Denial of responsibility for our role in the offense.* Sometimes the offense was a response to something we did. To forgive the offense, we must first admit to our own wrongdoing, maybe even repent of our part in the offense, before we can forgive the retaliation launched against us.

Admission is incredibly difficult. Not only does it require us to take responsibility for our actions and responses, but it also requires us to admit some responsibility for the action taken against us in retribution. It requires something many Christians should be good at practicing, but are not: humility.

As discussed earlier, humility plays a major role in forgiveness and repentance. The old adage "Pride goes before a fall" is saying just that. To properly forgive or repent, we must be humble. We must be able to acknowledge the fact we make mistakes, too. We must be able to appreciate all people as equal to us, even those not equal on an educational, arbitrarily societal, or economic scale. Such is not a common virtue, and those who practice it are discussed in saint-like terms: Mother Teresa, the Dali Lama, and Jimmy Carter are just a few. For such a prized virtue, its practice is not popular.

We must approach prayer with a willing intention as well as openness to obeying the Holy Spirit's guidance. In this way, we will be able to have the humility to see ourselves as we are and do something about it. Seeing ourselves as we are can be a very humbling experience, but it is the only way to get past this obstacle to forgiveness.

*Misunderstanding the role of forgiveness in the circumstance.* Sometimes we don't realize forgiveness (or repentance) is needed to resolve a problem. We don't recognize our anger or we don't realize we have hurt someone. To get past this obstacle, we must have an active prayer life, including a time of listening to God. A good practice is to check for issues in our daily lives using the Consciousness Examen.

The goal of the Consciousness Examen is to look at our day through God's eyes for issues we need to address. An established practice of morning and evening prayer, especially with a journal or notepad nearby to jot down insights brought to your mind by the Spirit of Christ residing within us, is invaluable to the Christian Disciple.

Another good practice before you go to bed is to pray for the people and events of the day. If you feel a tug in your heart for anyone you pray for, spend some extra time praying for and about that person. Be open to what you are experiencing about them. You will be prepared to be open and forgiving of others if you do this.

*Self-preservation or protection.* When we feel we are in danger or under attack, it is difficult to forgive. Especially when the person involved is dangerous, continuously attacking us, or unrepentant. There are many levels where this can be true from the vicious gossip or the abusive bully to the serial rapist or murderer. How do we forgive when we are living in fear or dread of the other person? How do we forgive while protecting ourselves?

Much of this resistance is tied to *misunderstanding the meaning of reconciliation.* If we equate forgiveness with reconciliation, it is understandable we would not want to forgive someone who is endangering our lives. However, forgiveness and reconciliation are not the same things.

When we forgive, we release ourselves from the burden of anger, hatred, pain, and fear inflicted on us by the actions of another. We do this by turning the circumstances over to God. As said earlier, reconciliation is a two-way activity involving both forgiveness and repentance. Unless both of these actions are entered into sincerely, reconciliation cannot take place.

To emphasize my point: If you are forgiving of someone who is truly repentant, who has taken action to recompense you for damages, who has taken action to get professional help, who has turned themselves over to authorities, or who has honored your wishes to keep their distance from you; only then can reconciliation take place. If you are forgiving of someone who has not taken major steps towards repentance, there can be no reconciliation.

I am not talking about some empty apology here. I am talking sincere repentance; the kind of repentance that feels compassion for the victims of their actions, seeks restoration of property, restitution of losses, and assistance in preventing a recurrence of the offense. When necessary, the offending individual takes steps to make sure the situation never happens again either by getting counseling, entering a 12-step program, turning themselves over to authorities, or receiving other professional help for their problems. In short, they are taking full responsibility for their actions. There may be repeat offenses, but they become fewer and farther between because the person is getting help to stop and taking action to distance themselves from their temptations.

There are many obstacles to forgiving. These are only a few common examples. If you are having trouble forgiving, sit with these obstacles and see if you can locate the source of your resistance.

**Exercises**

- Continue to set aside time for the Consciousness Examen each evening or morning for the next 30 days, making notes of what comes up. Let the theme of your meditations be to improve your ability to forgive and repent. While other things may come up, the specified theme will be brought more and more to your attention. At the end of the 30 days, review your notes to recognize how much closer you have grown to God.

- Practice the Lord's Prayer as outlined in Appendix B. Set a time length of three to five minutes per section. However, modify the prayer when you reach the sections on forgiving and repenting so that they are twice as long as the other sections. Make a determined effort to keep your mind open to what ever comes. Let the Spirit breath through your prayer. Perhaps incorporate the Jesus Prayer as part of this section if you have trouble staying with it.

# Obstacles to Repentance

*"Now I rejoice, not because you were grieved, but because your grief led to repentance; for you felt a godly grief, so that you were not harmed in any way by us. For godly grief produces a repentance that leads to salvation and brings no regret, but worldly grief produces death." II Corinthians 7:9-10*

According to II Corinthians 7:9-10, coming to an understanding of your faults leads to grief. However, grief that leads to repentance is a pain over which we can rejoice because this kind of grief is "godly grief". In other words, this is grief when acted upon brings you closer to God, to salvation, to life. "Worldly grief" or grief that is not acted upon in repentance but is allowed to fester in one's heart will lead to death. "Godly grief" may hurt, but it does no harm. Indeed, it heals our relationship with God. "Worldly grief" hurts us to death because it separates us from God. Anything that separates us from God is sin and leads to death.

Repentance is very similar to forgiveness. Many of the characteristics needed to forgive are also needed to repent: humility, love, the need to be freed from a terrible situation, the desire to be brought closer to God, the desire to restore relationships, and to release sorrow (or "grief") about the situation. There is one more besides—the burning desire to undo what you have done and, where this is not possible, to make reparations or act in some way that will mitigate further damages.

Please note: You cannot obtain reconciliation if the offended party does not forgive you. That may hurt, but remember, they must be allowed to deal with their issues just as you must be allowed to deal with yours. Your task is to be prepared to respond with repentance when the injured party is ready to receive it. In the meantime, do everything you can to mitigate the damages resulting from your offense. Such work and acceptance of responsibility could go a long way towards reducing the other person's fear of further injury and allow them to forgive you.

There are blocks to repentance just as there are to forgiveness.

- You didn't know someone was offended
- Excusing or justifying your actions by:
    - Attributing them to bad parenting, environment, or lack of schooling
    - Your actions were not intended to offend
    - Declaring the offended person to be too sensitive
    - The "He/She hit me first" defense
    - They are one of "those" people, groups, or classes
- An inability to forgive yourself
- Denial of responsibility for your role in the offense:
    - The magnitude of the offense is too overwhelming
    - The thought of the extent of the punishment, retribution, or restitution frightens you
    - You were just following the crowd
- Misunderstanding the role of forgiveness in the circumstance
- Misunderstanding the meaning of reconciliation

Let's look at each of these in some detail.

*Didn't know someone was offended.* Here is where a regular practice of the prayer form, Consciousness Examen, comes into play. If you have unknowingly offended someone, and you are practicing Consciousness Examen each day, the Holy Spirit will bring to your mind times you may have unknowingly hurt someone. You will find yourself reviewing an event during the day and remember maybe a sudden cool attitude towards you from a friend or the expression on someone's face registering pain or shock of some kind. Write it down and decide how you will address the situation. If they are someone you see every day, stop by the next day and say, "I was praying or thinking about my day yesterday and thought I might have hurt your feelings when I said.... If I did, I want to apologize. I certainly did not mean it that way." You can also phone the person or send them a short note if you don't see the person all the time.

One more thing: If the offense occurred before a group of people, apologize in front of that group. Such an apology reflects the sincerity of the apology and provides automatic restitution of the offended person's reputation before the group, as well as your own. While this should not be the reason for the apology, you will also be perceived by the group as someone people can trust to be honest and responsible for their actions. They will know as a child once defined love; their "name is safe in your mouth."

*Excusing or justifying our actions by attributing them to bad parenting, environment, or lack of schooling.* Any and all of these things may be true of you and psychologists have been known to put these up as a defense in court to reduce jail terms, but they are just that... excuses. There are many people in the world who have survived terrible life situations and become successful and honorable members of society. If you wish to escape the effects of any of these life situations, you can get the help you need to change them. Never use them as an excuse for offensive behavior unless you add to your explanation the statement you are actively working to correct this behavior.

*Your actions were not intended to offend.* One oft-repeated tenet of Neuro-Linguistic Programming is "The meaning of any communication is the response you get." If the response you received is not the one you hoped for, if it has obviously offended people, apologize and restate your message in a different way. If you don't understand why what you said or did was offensive, get some feedback from a trusted source; preferably someone representative of the people you are trying to reach.

*Declaring the offended person to be too sensitive.* This statement may be true. However, in the interests of a peaceful relationship with someone, you should apologize for it just the same. Just make a mental note to watch how you treat or speak to this person in the future. If this hypersensitivity becomes an on-going issue in your relationship you might try, as much as possible to distance yourself from this person in the future. I am not advocating lying, submitting to unfair situations, or making yourself a martyr. If it is not possible to discuss an issue with the person, get a mediator. If that is not possible or does not help, about all you can do is distance yourself.

It is important to take into account your way of dealing with people. If you have a tendency to tease people "all in good fun, of course"; come on too loud or too strong, or are borderline aggressive in your communications; the seemingly "easily offended person" may be tired of being the focus of your jokes, or confronted by your manner. Perhaps they have been targeted by bullies in the past, in which case your manner could easily be mistaken for further abuse. Apologize and tone down your mannerisms a little when dealing with that person in the future.

*The "He/She hit me first" defense:* This was a frequently heard defense in my parent's car as my five siblings, and I were growing up. It takes on different forms with adults. Anytime we justify our actions because of the treatment we received; we are making this defense. It is a strange defense. Essentially, you are saying your actions are justifiable because the other person is treating you the same way. That is never a good defense. Romans 12:19-21 tells us:

> *"Beloved, never avenge yourselves, but leave room for the wrath of God; for it is written, 'Vengeance is mine, I will repay, says the Lord.' No, 'if your enemies are hungry, feed them; if they are thirsty, give them something to drink; for by doing this you will heap burning coals on their heads.' Do not be overcome by evil, but overcome evil with good."*

## The Unforgivable Sin

My mother once asked my grandmother, Sarah Shedd, how she could be so unfailingly kind in her care of her sisters-in-law. These sisters-in-law were elderly and Sarah was their only caretaker. They were constantly criticizing and complaining about everything she did. Sarah told my mother, "I decided how I wanted to treat people many years ago. The fact that someone else is treating me badly does not change that. I won't let anyone bring me down to their level."

*They are one of "those" people, groups, or classes.* Excusing your treatment of someone else because of their age, race, sex, gender identity, economic status, religion, appearance, handicap, or any other defining characteristic is discrimination. Apologize and make restitution as quickly as possible. There is no defense for this kind of behavior. This area includes bullying. When you find yourself reacting to a person because of who they are, make an extra effort to get to know them, familiarize yourself with their condition, or get professional help to overcome your prejudice.

One important step for you could be getting to know or confront the cultural and social mores that were a common part of your life growing up. These are difficult to see clearly because we are all raised with a set of glasses controlling how we see the world. Some of these glasses are good, but many are not. To become familiar with your own set of glasses, randomly select people in a public setting and ask yourself what you think of that person. If you find yourself making assumptions, just by looking at them, about the person's intelligence, their ability to hold a job, or their love and care for their family; you may have a social disease known as prejudice. Definitely find some way to cross this ignorance barrier.

*Inability to forgive yourself.* If we cannot forgive ourselves how can we believe someone else can forgive us? If you are in this place in the forgiveness and repentance process, repent just the same. Then pray. Not being able to forgive yourself can cause you to be unreceptive to God's forgiveness when it is offered. It makes all relationships impossible. Think about the old line from Groucho Marx, "I refuse to join any club that would have me as a member." While funny when Groucho says it, this is a self-deprecating and self-destructive attitude. Learn to love yourself and you will find loving others easier.

*Denial of responsibility for your role in the offense. The magnitude of the offense is too overwhelming.* It may be a car accident that kills someone, an error in judgment that causes financial ruin for another, or maybe you participated in a group that ended up doing something illegal. Whatever it was, your participation in the action still requires your repentance despite your ignorance of the consequences or the accidental nature of the offense. Your participation in the action is the key. If you are in denial about your role in any offense, pray about it. If you are not accepting responsibility for an offense you need to set right, it will affect your relationship to God. Matthew 5:21-24 says:

> "You have heard that it was said to those of ancient times, 'You shall not murder'; and 'whoever murders shall be liable to judgment.' But I say to you that if you are angry with a brother or sister, you will be liable to judgment; and if you insult a brother or sister, you will be liable to the council; and if you say, 'You fool,' you will be liable to the hell of fire. So when you are offering your gift at the altar, if you remember that your brother or sister has something against you, leave your gift there before the altar and go; first be reconciled to your brother or sister, and then come and offer your gift."

Your relationship with God is seriously compromised by unrepentance as well as unforgiveness, and not just unrepentance before God, but also unrepentance with your fellow human beings. Pray about it. Make Consciousness Examen a critical part of your prayer life. This prayer is invaluable in maintaining your relationship with God.

*The thought of the extent of the punishment, retribution, or restitution frightens you.* As a child, we have all been through this. We do something and know we will be punished by parent, neighbor, or teacher. We know we are "in for it." So, we try to cover it up: lie; hide our responsibility for the misdeed, blame someone else, and hope no one notices. It's a primal reaction; an attempt at self-preservation. The effort may be instinctual, but it should not be tolerated. Practice courage! While it may not seem like it at the time, coming clean is not as stressful as living with the knowledge and guilt of wrongdoing, the prospect of punishment, as well as its destructive influence on your relationships. Admitting wrong and doing all you can to set it right will bring you peace even when experiencing punishment. You no longer have pending discovery and judgment hanging over your head.

*You were just following the crowd.* We have all done this at one time or another in our lives. We tell the patrolman who pulled us over for speeding, "I was just trying to keep up with traffic." We are all familiar with the defense, "But everyone else was doing it!" as well as the response, "If everyone was jumping off a cliff, would you do it?" Herd mentality is an animal behavior. However, we are different from animals. It only takes one person, standing up for what they believe, to begin to sway the multitude by offering another choice. An example of what I mean: One young man I know, a senior in high school was discussing with classmates where they would go after the prom. Another classmate said his father had bought a keg, and everyone was invited, even though all were under drinking age. My young friend said he thought he and his date would run down to a small, all-night diner by the interstate and have breakfast. Nearly the entire class joined him. The little diner was not prepared for such a huge crowd, so the young people took their own orders, served themselves, and bused their own tables. They spent the rest of their night there working, visiting, and laughing together. I doubt any of them ever forgot it.

Going along with the crowd may be easy at the time, but the results could well ruin your life. There are many stories of peer pressure activities gone wrong: gang membership initiations requiring drive-by shootings being one clear example. Even when our actions are part of a group, we are accountable for what we do. Even when the group does not follow our lead, we are expected to live our lives consciously and responsibly. We still face God alone in our accountability. When we are part of a group, we would do well to have the courage illustrated by the words of Ralph Waldo Emerson:

> "It is easy in the world to live after the world's opinion; it is easy in solitude to live after our own; but the great man [or woman] is he [she] who in the midst of the crowd keeps with perfect

> sweetness the independence of solitude." from *The Complete Prose Works of Ralph Waldo Emerson*

*Misunderstanding the role of forgiveness in the situation.* Repentance is our responsibility. It is not dependent on whether or not the injured party forgives us. We are still required to repent. Just as those who have been injured have a responsibility to forgive whether their offender repents or not, we have the responsibility to repent whether or not we are forgiven by the offended party. Part of repentance is restitution. How this might look in real life varies depending on the offense and the openness of the offended party to receive that restitution.

Many people rank sin by degrees of sin. I understand degrees of sin from the context of restitution. Compensating people for monetary loss and hardships is a fairly easy thing to do. Compensating someone for the loss of their life or the life of a loved one is impossible to do.

There is also a special reference in scripture to those who harm children, and I would include in that category those who are childlike due to mental conditions. Matthew 18:5-7 tells us:

> "Whoever welcomes one such child in my name welcomes me. If any of you put a stumbling block before one of these little ones who believe in me, it would be better for you if a great millstone were fastened around your neck and you were drowned in the depth of the sea. Woe to the world because of stumbling blocks! Occasions for stumbling are bound to come, but woe to the one by whom the stumbling block comes!"

When we abuse or kill children, bully them, prevent them from receiving the basic needs of life, prevent them from receiving an education, abandon them (either in reality or by neglect), or introduce them to violence in such a way as to lead them to believe this is a normal way to live; we are imposing stumbling blocks in their paths. The above scripture says we are better off dead if we do such things. Not only because they are helpless to defend themselves, but, because, as the world learns more about the upbringing of children, we realize environmental factors play an important role in how children respond to their world. While some can rise above these factors, they seem to be the exception. When a child is raised in the midst of poverty, racism, and abuse; why do we wonder when they join gangs? Why do we wonder when they bully and hurt other children? Why do we wonder when they become criminals? All of these actions lay an unfair burden of repentance and forgiveness on the injured child.

How a society treats its weakest members is an indicator of that society's health as well as its Christian witness. Restitution is nearly impossible and requires much patience in such cases.

If there is a case for all sin being a mortal sin, it is this: we do not know how our actions affect another human being. Some people think verbal abuse (name-calling, teasing) is not as damaging as other forms, yet it is a form of bullying repeatedly resulting in suicide. How do you make restitution for such responses to your actions?

*Misunderstanding the meaning of reconciliation.* I have said this before, and I say it again here, forgiveness alone and repentance alone do not constitute reconciliation. What they do is prepare the garden of your heart to receive the forgiveness or repentance when it comes. If you attempt to force reconciliation before the other party is ready, you are committing an offense against them. You may still feel guilty because the other party has not forgiven you. If so, don't blame them. Make it a matter of prayer until they are open to respond to your repentance with forgiveness. To do anything else is to perpetuate the offense in a different form bordering on bullying and judgment. You have no idea how deep your seemingly minor offense may have cut the other person. Give them space to forgive you and do not attempt to assuage your guilt with frequent statements and scripture quotes about being a forgiving Christian. You could drive them from the church, and your last offense will be worse than your first.

## Exercises

Note: These prayers are the same as the prayers in the prior section. This has been done intentionally due to the powerful properties of transformation contained in these prayers. Please practice them with respect and expectation.

- Continue to set aside time for the Consciousness Examen each evening or morning for the next 30 days, making notes of what comes up. Let the theme of your meditations be to improve your ability to forgive and repent. While other things may come up, the specified theme will be brought more and more to your attention. At the end of the 30 days, review your notes to recognize how much closer you have grown to God.

- Practice the Lord's Prayer as outlined in Appendix B. Set a time length of three to five minutes per section. However, modify the prayer when you reach the sections on forgiving and repenting so that they are twice as long as the other sections. Make a determined effort to keep your mind open to what ever comes. Let the Spirit breath through your prayer. Perhaps incorporate the Jesus Prayer as part of this section if you have trouble staying with it.

# Other Issues Interfering with Forgiveness and Repentance

*"And do not grieve the Holy Spirit of God, with which you were marked with a seal for the day of redemption. Put away from you all bitterness and wrath and anger and wrangling and slander, together with all malice, and be kind to one another, tenderhearted, forgiving one another, as God in Christ has forgiven you." Ephesians 4:30-32*

Ephesians 4:30-32 speaks of purging yourself of a habit of fighting, arguing, and negativity. Instead, we are to develop a habit of kindness, loving care, and forgiveness towards each other. Will this make us more vulnerable? Yes. Will it allow us to see more good in the world? Absolutely. Will it bring us closer to God? Indeed! Will it help us be more forgiving of each other's shortcomings? It will.

If you find similar opportunities for offense repeatedly arising in your life the problem may be you have never completely and truly cleared up a similar, original offense by either forgiving or repenting.

To illustrate what I mean, let's say you repeatedly find yourself a victim of bullies; through grade school, high school, college, and now at the office. Or you continually find yourself surrounded by idiots you have to keep in line. These have become patterns of interaction in your life whether you are consciously aware of them or not. To release such patterns, you must begin with the first incident, the initiating pattern. You will need to forgive the first bully or repent the way you treat people. (No, it doesn't matter if you think they really are idiots. You don't treat people like that.) Be sensitive to where your prayer leads you. Especially if it is leading you to confronting the bully with forgiveness or providing an apology or some form of restitution.

This process is like going to the dentist to have your teeth cleaned and finding out you need a root canal. The deeper and longer the pattern has gone on, the more time it will take to resolve the past and extract yourself from it. Going deep with long patience will help release you from these patterns. You may need assistance from a professional counselor. Role playing alternative patterns of behavior in similar situations can also be helpful.

For most of my life, I have found myself a victim of people who were not sane. Ranging from simple OCD problems to sociopaths, they seemed to be everywhere, at times. I needed to learn something from these interactions or I would continually find these people surfacing in my life. It was not until I learned the lesson of dealing with these people that they stopped showing up. I learned: Just because someone is going into a crazy space does not mean I have to follow. I learned how to stay calm and present with the situation without becoming reactive to their rants. It was only in this way, I was able to find some peace when dealing with these sad people.

Another issue few people concern themselves with is the ripple effect of their actions. Let's say your refusal to forgive or repent has caused you so much stress you have developed a chronic condition. It can be anything from an anxiety disorder to cancer. Or maybe your lack of forgiveness or lack of repentance has caused you to resort to a habitual dysfunctional behavior of forcing others to side with you or be treated as your enemy as well. You need to forgive yourself for this and release your friends, families, and co-workers from the bonds your rage has placed on them.

Our offenses are like a stone dropped in water; rippling out from the person with whom we are struggling and spreading outward to your and their extended family, friends, and co-workers. It is the old story of the boss yelling at the employee, the employee going home and yelling at their spouse, the spouse yelling at their child, the child yelling at the dog, who then bites the mailman. We may not see the entire fallout of pain we have caused, but we will be held responsible for it nonetheless.

So our repentance and forgiveness must include an umbrella prayer, which, like umbrella insurance, includes the unforeseen consequences of our actions. Use the Lord's Prayer for this, or Using Art meditation. Both work well here.

## Exercises

Note: These prayers are the same as the prayers in the prior section. This has been done intentionally due to the powerful properties of transformation contained in these prayers. Please practice them with respect and expectation.

- Continue to set aside time for the Consciousness Examen each evening or morning for the next 30 days, making notes of what comes up. Let the theme of your meditations be to improve your ability to forgive and repent. While other things may come up, the specified theme will be brought more and more to your attention. At the end of the 30 days, review your notes to recognize how much closer you have grown to God.

- Practice the Lord's Prayer as outlined in Appendix B. Set a time length of three to five minutes per section. However, modify the prayer when you reach the sections on forgiving and repenting so that they are twice as long as the other sections. Make a determined effort to keep your mind open to what ever comes. Let the Spirit breath through your prayer. Perhaps incorporate the Jesus Prayer as part of this section if you have trouble staying with it.

# Reconciliation

*"From now on, therefore, we regard no one from a human point of view; even though we once knew Christ from a human point of view, we know him no longer in that way. So if anyone is in Christ, there is a new creation: everything old has passed away; see, everything has become new! All this is from God, who reconciled us to himself through Christ, and has given us the ministry of reconciliation; that is, in Christ God was reconciling the world to himself, not counting their trespasses against them, and entrusting the message of reconciliation to us. II Corinthians 5:16-19*

Reconciliation is a state of peace. It happens when we have truly forgiven and truly repented for the actions which forced the separation between ourselves and another. A state of peace is created to the point where we can live in harmony, even friendship, once more.

Furthermore, practicing forgiveness and repentance each time it is needed prepares your heart as a place for the Spirit of God to reside or, more to the point, for you to acknowledge and answer the call of God in your heart. Unforgiveness and unrepentance are sin. This sin separates us from God in a way more obvious sin does not. This sin hides from us and can even be seen as righteous in our sight. After all, they are in the wrong so we are right to hold them accountable. Or they are too sensitive, petty, or in some way so much less than we are—So many excuses!

We don't understand the effect unforgiveness and unrepentance has on our relationship with God. God made us to learn from experience. Practicing forgiveness and repentance will strengthen our faith in the mercy and grace of God.

We learn by experience. We may learn things from books, from the experiences of others, and through prayer. However, in the area of reconciliation, we must learn about forgiveness and repentance through our personal practice of these virtues. It is important we learn the virtues of forgiveness and repentance because, one day, we will come before God, fully seeing our lives as God sees them without being able to ignore our actions or make excuses for them the way we do in this secular world. If we have practiced forgiveness and repentance in our lives, we will be more able to repent our actions and know God can forgive them. If we do not practice forgiveness and repentance, we will believe there are things that cannot be forgiven and turn away from God. It will not be that God does not forgive us. It will be we do not believe we can be forgiven.

That is the crux of the reason why the lack of forgiveness and repentance is the unforgivable sin. We learn by doing. Our faith grows through our experiences. If we cannot forgive something or believe something cannot be forgiven, we will not believe God can forgive us and will not accept when God offers us forgiveness. We will become so lost in our own guilt and pain, we will not even realize forgiveness is being offered or believe it could be offered. Like the small children we are, we will hide from God for fear of being consumed by his glory and righteous judgment.

Forgiveness and Repentance are not unforgivable sins because God cannot forgive them! They are unforgivable sins because we can neither perform the repentance required nor accept the forgiveness offered. Essentially, we have come to believe there are things that cannot be forgiven. We have come to believe forgiveness from God is impossible.

In the end, the confrontation by God is called "judgment" for lack of a better word. In reality, we come face to face with who we are as God sees us. When confronted with the holiness of God and the littleness of ourselves in God's eyes, we judge ourselves and turn our backs on God. That is what the scripture passage means in Luke 6:36-37:

> *"Be merciful, just as your Father is merciful. 'Do not judge, and you will not be judged; do not condemn, and you will not be condemned. Forgive, and you will be forgiven;'"*

When we turn away from God, God's mercy allows us to go to a place God has prepared for us so we may be as comfortable as possible. But we cannot forget what we have seen in God's presence. We cannot forget the truth of God's confrontation. We will not be allowed to languish in our excuses and rhetoric any longer. The hell we find will be of our making; the Lake of Fire created by our own anguish produced by our own guilt.

When my church (Community of Christ) began to ordain women, one of my uncles, Lyle Shedd, could not accept this change and left the church to join a group of others like himself. This group held a lot of animosity towards the church and took every opportunity to go on the attack. Many of them broke off from family and life-long friends who did not leave the church. My Uncle Lyle did not do this. He was sad his family had not followed him out of the church, but he was the same father and husband to them and uncle to me I had always known. He even mentored me when I was about to perform my first wedding!

My uncle contracted leukemia. He fought it for many years, but it eventually claimed his life. My most powerful memory of him was during a visit with him a week before his death. My family had received the word he was failing, so we made the trip to see him and say goodbye. His bedroom was a large room, filled with family visiting and laughing together over old times. We each got a chance to sit with Lyle and visit for a few minutes.

When my turn came, we talked quietly for a few minutes, then he pointed to the family all around us and said, "You know, Mikal, we spend so much of our time worrying about the little things, making them so big, so important. But this is the all and only thing that is important, the love we have for each other. And it is the only thing we take with us."

I will never forget him or what he told me that day.

When I hear people speak of heaven or hell as a physical reality made of all the "things" they didn't have on earth, I am both concerned and amused. Because the "things" they dream of are much lesser things then the things of God. They are so much less than the reality of God.

Jesus' appearances to his disciples were met with fear because they thought he was a ghost. They thought he was dead and had walked through the walls because he was not substantial. Yet he ate and drank like they did. The truth is not that Jesus was a ghost. The truth is Jesus was more substantial than the walls he passed through. In many ways, the beings we are and the things we value are ghosts. The science of Physics has found we are made up mostly of small bits of matter joined together by large quantities of empty space filled with an energy they cannot identify. Scripture tells us God is in and around and through everything, making us all one. It is time we began seeing the world in this way.

We won't think about those "things" we hold dear today or even want them where we are going. The true heaven will be about fully reconciled relationships, allowing us to become one with God and each other. The true hell will be built from shattered excuses and a knowing, even an empathetic experiencing, of the effects of our actions.

**Exercises**

- Continue to set aside time for the Consciousness Examen each evening or morning for the next 30 days, making notes of what comes up. Let the theme of your meditations be to improve your ability to forgive and repent. While other things may come up, the specified theme will be brought more and more to your attention. At the end of the 30 days, review your notes to recognize how much closer you have grown to God.
- Using Lectio Divina meditate on II Corinthians 5:16-19, ask the Spirit to help you understand better the relationship between forgiveness, repentance, reconciliation, and your relationship with God.

# What We Must Do

"And all who have this hope in him purify themselves, just as he is pure. Everyone who commits sin is guilty of lawlessness; sin is lawlessness. You know that he was revealed to take away sins, and in him there is no sin. No one who abides in him sins; no one who sins has either seen him or known him. Little children, let no one deceive you. Everyone who does what is right is righteous, just as he is righteous. Everyone who commits sin is a child of the devil; for the devil has been sinning from the beginning. The Son of God was revealed for this purpose, to destroy the works of the devil. Those who have been born of God do not sin, because God's seed abides in them; they cannot sin, because they have been born of God The children of God and the children of the devil are revealed in this way: all who do not do what is right are not from God, nor are those who do not love their brothers and sisters. For this is the message you have heard from the beginning, that we should love one another." I John 3:3-11

I John 3:3-11 declares the relationship between God and those who constitute God's people. This scripture also declares the relationship

## The Unforgivable Sin

between God and those who commit sins. It also tells us how to tell which kind of person we are: if we do not do what is right or do not love each other, we are not from God.

So, how do we stay aware of the times we need to forgive, repent, or, in many cases, both? How do we make sure we are right with God?

Here are some daily practices I find helpful.

First: Every time I hear myself say, "That is unforgivable!" alarm bells go off in my head. Immediately, I repent that statement in prayer and ask for help to make it untrue in my life.

Second: I practice Consciousness Examen each evening before going to bed. Sometimes it just takes a few minutes; sometimes longer, but I have asked the Holy Spirit to bring to mind the things happening during that day I need to remember. I keep a journal so I can write these things down and act upon them the next day or, sometimes, immediately. A notepad and pen will do just as well if you don't keep a journal.

To be successful, I pray with the intention of acting upon what I receive during this meditative practice. Then I follow through. If you pray any prayer with the intention of acting on what you receive, and create a pattern of acting on what you receive, your prayer will be much more powerful, the answers much more forthcoming. Many times, I have received an answer I could not see myself acting upon and finding myself, like Moses, making excuses as to why I cannot do what is asked of me. At such times, I pray for courage and faith to do what is being asked of me. I always receive help to fulfill God's commands and come away from the experience in awe and with stronger faith.

Third: Take action! Actively practice forgiving and repenting as soon as you are aware of the need to do so. If you practice the Consciousness Examen on a regular basis, you will eventually move from awareness at the end of the day during your prayer time to awareness at the time of the action.

Fourth: Pray! You cannot change if you do not make your life a matter of prayer. You cannot grow closer to God if you do not pray about everything. The more you pray, the closer you grow to God, the easier it is to forgive and repent. It sets you free from the pride that interferes with forgiveness and repentance. You begin to find yourself difficult to offend. Your relationships grow stronger. Your stress and anxiety go down. A good format for prayer is the Lord's Prayer. I am not talking about a recitation of the scripture. I am talking about the use of the prayer as the actual template for prayer it was meant to be.

Some helpful tools for releasing your anger and preparing for forgiving or repenting include:

- Praying for the offending party and your ability to forgive them. If you feel no desire to forgive, pray for the desire to forgive. As it says in Matthew 5:43-46:

    *"You have heard that it was said, 'You shall love your neighbor and hate your enemy.' But I say to you, Love your enemies and pray for those who persecute you so that you may be children of your Father in heaven; for he makes his sun rise on the evil and on the good, and sends rain on the righteous and the unrighteous. For if you love those who love you, what reward do you have? Do not even the tax-collectors do the same?"*

- Write a letter to the offending party. (Don't mail it!)
- Pray the Lord's Prayer, daily
- Express your feelings through artwork.
- Walking meditations such as walking a labyrinth.
- Look for the good things that have come out of the offense. Maybe you were able to meet a new friend. Maybe you gained a better understanding of yourself. Maybe you are finally able to see the offending party, for who they are and can agree to go your separate ways. Maybe the only good thing to come out of it is an exercise in forgiving or repenting. Maybe you have become a teacher, teaching others how to avoid or handle such incidents in the future. Just remember, when you are dealing with God, you will always grow from the incident.
- Find something each day to be thankful for in your current situation.

When we practice these actions and attitudes each day, we set ourselves free of the terrible burdens unforgiveness and unrepentance lay upon us.

## Exercises

- Continue to set aside time for the Consciousness Examen each evening or morning for the next 30 days, making notes of what comes up. Let the theme of your meditations be to improve your ability to forgive and repent. While other things may come up, the specified theme will be brought more and more to your attention. At the end of the 30 days, review your notes to recognize how much closer you have grown to God.

- Using Lectio Divina, meditate on I John 3:3-11, ask the Spirit to help you understand better the relationship between forgiveness, repentance, reconciliation, and your relationship with God.

- Plan a daily prayer practice and scripture study. Use some of the suggestions in this chapter for guidance, but it must be your own plan, fitting your life, or you won't stay with it. If you miss a day, come back to it the next. Don't beat yourself up about it, just take a deep breath, let it out, and set up some kind of a reminder so you don't forget again. Something that may help is to perform a monthly or weekly review of your journal or notes to notice how far you have come. Realizing prayer is a blessing to your life instead of a burden will help you stay with it.

# APPENDIX A

### Scripture Passages Grounding the Text

Matthew 5:21-25 "'You have heard that it was said to those of ancient times, You shall not murder; and whoever murders shall be liable to judgment. But I say to you that if you are angry with a brother or sister, you will be liable to judgment; and if you insult a brother or sister, you will be liable to the council; and if you say, 'You fool,' you will be liable to the hell of fire.' So when you are offering your gift at the altar, if you remember that your brother or sister has something against you, leave your gift there before the altar and go; first be reconciled to your brother or sister, and then come and offer your gift. Come to terms quickly with your accuser while you are on the way to court with him, or your accuser may hand you over to the judge, and the judge to the guard, and you will be thrown into prison."

Matthew 38-41 "You have heard that it was said, 'An eye for an eye and a tooth for a tooth.' But I say to you, Do not resist an evildoer. But if anyone strikes you on the right cheek, turn the other also; and if anyone wants to sue you and take your coat, give your cloak as well; and if anyone forces you to go one mile, go also the second mile."

Matthew 5:43-46 "You have heard that it was said, 'You shall love your neighbor and hate your enemy.' But I say to you, Love your enemies and pray for those who persecute you, so that you may be children of your Father in heaven; for he makes his sun rise on the evil and on the good, and sends rain on the righteous and on the unrighteous. For if you love those who love you, what reward do you have? Do not even the tax collectors do the same?"

Matthew 6:9-15 "Pray then in this way: Our Father in heaven, hallowed be your name. Your kingdom come. Your will be done, on earth as it is in heaven. Give us this day our daily bread. And forgive us our debts, as we also have forgiven our debtors. And do not bring us to the time of trial, but rescue us from the evil one. For if you forgive others their trespasses, your heavenly Father will also forgive you; but if you do not forgive others, neither will your Father forgive your trespasses."

Matthew 7:1-3 "Do not judge, so that you may not be judged. For with the judgment you make you will be judged, and the measure you give will be the measure you get. Why do you see the speck in your neighbor's eye, but do not notice the log in your own eye?"

Matthew 7:12 "In everything do to others as you would have them do to you; for this is the law and the prophets."

Matthew 12:31 "Therefore I tell you, people will be forgiven for every sin and blasphemy, but blasphemy against the Spirit will not be forgiven."

Matthew 18:5-7 "Whoever welcomes one such child in my name welcomes me. 'If any of you put a stumbling block before one of these little ones who believe in me, it would be better for you if a great millstone were fastened around your neck and you were drowned in the depth of the sea. Woe to the world because of stumbling blocks! Occasions for stumbling are bound to come, but woe to the one by whom the stumbling block comes!'"

Matthew 18:21-35 "Then Peter came and said to him, 'Lord, if another member of the church sins against me, how often should I forgive? As many as seven times?' Jesus said to him, 'Not seven times, but, I tell you, seventy-seven times. For this reason the kingdom of heaven may be compared to a king who wished to settle accounts with his slaves. When he began the reckoning, one who owed him ten thousand talents was brought to him; and, as he could not pay, his lord ordered him to be sold, together with his wife and children and all his possessions, and payment to be made. So the slave fell on his knees before him, saying, 'Have patience with me, and I will pay you everything.' And out of pity for him, the lord of that slave released him and forgave him the debt. But that same slave, as he went out, came upon one of his fellow slaves who owed him a hundred denarii; and seizing him by the throat, he said, 'Pay what you owe.' Then his fellow slave fell down and pleaded with him, 'Have patience with me, and I will pay you.' But he refused; then he went and threw him into prison until he would pay the debt. When his fellow slaves saw what had happened, they were greatly distressed, and they went and reported to their lord all that had taken place. Then his lord summoned him and said to him, 'You wicked slave! I forgave you all that debt because you pleaded with me. Should you not have had mercy on your fellow slave, as I had mercy on you?' And in anger his lord handed him over to be tortured until he would pay his entire debt. So my heavenly Father will also do to every one of you, if you do not forgive your brother or sister from your heart."

Matthew 25:31-46 "When the Son of Man comes in his glory, and all the angels with him, then he will sit on the throne of his glory. All the nations will be gathered before him, and he will separate people one from another as a shepherd separates the sheep from the goats, and he will put the sheep at his right hand and the goats at the left. Then the king will say to those at his right hand, 'Come, you that are blessed by my Father, inherit the kingdom prepared for you from the foundation of the world; for I was hungry and you gave me food, I was thirsty and you gave me something to drink, I was a stranger and you welcomed me, I was naked and you gave me clothing, I was sick and you took care of me, I was in prison and you visited me.' Then the righteous will answer him, 'Lord, when was it that we saw you hungry and gave you food, or thirsty and gave you something to drink? And when was it that we saw you a stranger and welcomed you, or naked and gave you clothing? And when was it that we saw you sick or in prison and visited you?' And the king will answer them, 'Truly I tell you, just as you did it to one of the least of these who are members of my family, you did it to me.' Then he will say to those at his left hand, 'You that are accursed, depart from me into the eternal fire prepared for the devil and his angels; for I was hungry and you gave me no food, I was thirsty and you gave me nothing to drink, I was a stranger and you did not welcome me, naked and you did not give me clothing, sick and in prison and you did not visit me.' Then they also will answer, 'Lord, when was it that we saw you hungry or thirsty or a stranger or naked or sick or in prison, and did not take care of you?' Then he will answer them, 'Truly I tell you, just as you did not do it to one of the least of these, you did not do it to me.' And these will go away into eternal punishment, but the righteous into eternal life."

Mark 3:29 "but whoever blasphemes against the Holy Spirit can never have forgiveness, but is guilty of an eternal sin—"

Luke 6:36-37 "Be merciful, just as your Father is merciful. Do not judge, and you will not be judged; do not condemn, and you will not be condemned. Forgive, and you will be forgiven;"

Luke 10:26-28 "He said to him, 'What is written in the law? What do you read there?' He answered, 'You shall love the Lord your God with all your heart, and with all your soul, and with all your strength, and with all your mind; and your neighbor as yourself.' And he said to him, 'You have given the right answer; do this, and you will live.'"

John 3:16-17 "For God so loved the world that he gave his only Son, so that everyone who believes in him may not perish but may have eternal life. Indeed, God did not send the Son into the world to condemn the world, but in order that the world might be saved through him."

John 7:24 "Do not judge by appearances, but judge with right judgment."

John 8:31-32 "Then Jesus said to the Jews who had believed in him, "If you continue in my word, you are truly my disciples; and you will know the truth, and the truth will make you free."

Romans 8:26-27 "Likewise the Spirit helps us in our weakness; for we do not know how to pray as we ought, but that very Spirit intercedes with sighs too deep for words. And God, who searches the heart, knows what is the mind of the Spirit, because the Spirit intercedes for the saints according to the will of God."

Romans 12:19-21 "Beloved, never avenge yourselves, but leave room for the wrath of God for it is written, 'Vengeance is mine, I will repay, says the Lord.' No, 'if your enemies are hungry, feed them; if they are thirsty, give them something to drink; for by doing this you will heap burning coals on their heads.' Do not be overcome by evil, but overcome evil with good."

2 Corinthians 5:16-19 "From now on, therefore, we regard no one from a human point of view; even though we once knew Christ from a human point of view, we know him no longer in that way. So if anyone is in Christ, there is a new creation: everything old has passed away; see, everything has become new! All this is from God, who reconciled us to himself through Christ, and has given us the ministry of reconciliation; that is, in Christ God was reconciling the world to himself, not counting their trespasses against them, and entrusting the message of reconciliation to us."

2 Corinthians 7:9-10 "Now I rejoice, not because you were grieved, but because your grief led to repentance; for you felt a godly grief, so that you were not harmed in any way by us. For godly grief produces a repentance that leads to salvation and brings no regret, but worldly grief produces death."

Ephesians 4:25-27 "So then, putting away falsehood, let all of us speak the truth to our neighbors, for we are members of one another. Be angry but do not sin; do not let the sun go down on your anger, and do not make room for the devil."

Ephesians 4:30-32 "And do not grieve the Holy Spirit of God, with which you were marked with a seal for the day of redemption. Put away from you all bitterness and wrath and anger and wrangling and slander, together with all malice, and be kind to one another, tenderhearted, forgiving one another, as God in Christ has forgiven you."

Ephesians 6:12 "For our struggle is not against enemies of blood and flesh, but against the rulers, against the authorities, against the cosmic powers of this present darkness, against the spiritual forces of evil in the heavenly places."

Philippians 1:6 "I am confident of this, that the one who began a good work among you will bring it to completion by the day of Jesus Christ."

I Thessalonians 5:15-22 "See that none of you repays evil for evil, but always seek to do good to one another and to all. Rejoice always, pray without ceasing, give thanks in all circumstances; for this is the will of God in Christ Jesus for you. Do not quench the Spirit. Do not despise the words of prophets, but test everything; hold fast to what is good; abstain from every form of evil."

1 John 3:9-11 "Those who have been born of God do not sin, because God's seed abides in them; they cannot sin, because they have been born of God. The children of God and the children of the devil are revealed in this way: all who do not do what is right are not from God, nor are those who do not love their brothers and sisters. For this is the message you have heard from the beginning, that we should love one another."

I John 4:19-21 "We love because he first loved us. Those who say, 'I love God,' and hate their brothers or sisters, are liars; for those who do not love a brother or sister whom they have seen, cannot love God whom they have not seen. The commandment we have from him is this: those who love God must love their brothers and sisters also."

# Appendix B

**Prayers included in the Section**

Preparing for Prayer – Please read first

Western Meditation – Meditatio

Contemplation – Contemplatio

Consciousness Examen

The Lord's Prayer

Lectio Divina or Divine Word

The Jesus Prayer (also known as The Prayer of the Heart)

Write a Letter

Using Artwork

Movement Meditations

Gratitude Practice

Visualization Practice

## *Preparing for Prayer*

If you are serious about prayer, you begin each prayer with preparation. Have some supplies on hand so you don't have to interrupt your prayer to get them. Have a glass of water handy or cup of tea or coffee in case you get thirsty or are feeling particularly tired. If you are ill, don't eliminate your prayer time as this is when you need prayer the most. If you are particularly unwell, The Jesus Prayer is short and very comforting.

Of course, any time and place is good for prayer and you really don't need any "supplies" to get started. However, it is best to make prayer as easy for yourself as possible or you won't stay with it. One of the practices that makes prayer easier is called anchoring. Our minds were created to do some things on autopilot. When we prepare for something in the same way each day, just the act of preparation alone will set us in the frame of mind for that activity. You see this in athletes, musicians, writers, artists, and dancers as they go through the same motions each time they are about start their activity. This is why some people love to sit in the same place at church each Sunday. It automatically prepares their minds for what they are about to do. The act of preparation takes their minds to that place where the activity begins. Consequently, when we use a specific practice for entering prayer and meditation, just the act of preparation, such as lighting the candle, donning a prayer shawl, or a special breathing pattern will automatically prepare us for prayer.

With supplies, less is more. You don't have to pick everything! Each person is different and your prayer preparation will be different. Some of us are artists, some are writers, some are musicians, and some of us need to move.

The following are suggestions for supplies you might want to have on hand:

- Journals. I keep four journals for prayer (but then, I'm a writer!):
    o A Prayer Journal for my personal conversations with God and tracking our relationship and my personal growth. I also record insights I've gained while praying and studying scripture.

*The Unforgivable Sin*

- A Review Journal. Each month, I review my Prayer Journal for insights, signs of growth, and information I've learned over the past month. Sometimes, It amazes me how easily I have forgotten these things that were so special at the time. I transfer all these into my Review Journal.

- A Prayer Request Journal tracks those people, concerns, and things you are currently praying for. A Prayer Request Journal serves several purposes:

    - It helps you to remember what you are praying for so nobody and nothing is forgotten in the press of daily life.

    - One day while reviewing my Prayer Journal, I realized God had answered one of my prayers in a rather amazing way, and I had not expressed thanks. A Prayer Request Journal prevents that from happening.

    - I leave a large space after each entry so I have room for the date of the answer to the prayer, room to write what the answer to the prayer was, and then praise God.

    - I date the entries in my Prayer Request Journal. In this way, I know how long I have been praying for a situation, person, or thing. When I have prayed for something longer than a month, I look at the prayer again in a meditative state of mind and ask the following questions. Please note: There is always a reason. God has never answered a sincere prayer request I have prayed according to God's will with, "No."

        - Was the prayer answered and I didn't know it? Maybe I need to check back with that person.

- Is the answer to my prayer awaiting some action on my part, but I don't know it or I am avoiding or procrastinating on it?

- Am I praying the wrong prayer for this person, situation, or thing? If so, how should I be praying? Do I need to rephrase it? (This is usually my problem.)

- Is the way I am praying against God's will in this matter? Is this a selfish prayer born of anger, greed, pride, or unforgiveness? God loves all of creation, including all the people in it. If you are praying for harm or for God to take sides against one of God's creatures, your prayer will not be answered. If you were to truthfully visualize God at the moment of your prayer, God would have His arms crossed and wearing that look your parents wore when they were thinking, "Huh? Really?"

- If I do need to change the way I'm praying for something:
    o I date the entry,
    o I write down why the prayer is being crossed off.
    o I praise God for teaching me how to pray better.
    o I write down the location of the corrected prayer, if any.
    o I cross off the old prayer in regular ink,

- Do I just need to be patient? There may be a lot of universe to move before your prayer can be answered.
- I make a note of any new lesson I have learned on prayer in my Prayer Journal so I won't forget it.
- When I realize a prayer has been answered:
  - I write down the date.
  - I write down the nature of the answer.
  - I thank God for the answer with praise and thanksgiving.
  - I ceremoniously cross it off with a non-bleeding colored marker. Then I can flip through the Prayer Request Journal when I'm struggling. I can see all the answers to prayer and it renews my faith.

o A Gratitude Journal – I write in this at the end of each day. There are several ways to keep a Gratitude Journal:
- Write down five things each day you are grateful for.
- Write down one thing each day you are grateful for. Expand on it. Explain why you are grateful and express praise for this thing.
- Track expressions of praise. This tends to be more like a scrapbook than a journal. I date the entry and write down how it came to me.
  - A poem that makes your heart sing
  - A hymn that lifted your Spirit
  - An expression of thanks you received for something you did.

- A picture of something glorious
- Joy over a breakthrough in your faith and understanding.
- Anything that brings out the praise side of your soul.

- Pens, pencils, markers, art supplies, glue, tape, pretty pictures for collage, decorative embellishments, stickers, paint
- Drawing or artist papers
- Sticky notes or a notebook for notes to take with you into the day.
- A lap desk
- Candles, incense, flowers
- Meditation CDs and CD player
- A beautiful picture
- Walking or running shoes, jacket, umbrella
- A timer

You will notice as you go through the following prayers, some are recommended for a certain time of day. The Consciousness Examen can be done at any time, even as part of another prayer. However, it is most effective as an end-of-day meditation because it strives to comprehend God's understanding of the transactions of your day. The Lord's Prayer also can be done any time of the day. However, it is most effective as a beginning-of-day meditation because certain features are addressing the coming day.

Use these prayers as you feel lead. In the end, praying is a fostering of your personal relationship with God and only you and God know what will do that.

May God bless your efforts to move toward Him.

## Western Meditation - Meditatio

This is a time of quiet, set aside to think about a particular subject or question weighing on your mind or for which you have been studying. You have reached a point where you are needing divine guidance or wisdom. It is similar to Eastern Meditation in that you are quieting your mind, but the goal is different. Both forms of meditation require quieting and emptying the mind which is why translators adopted the term meditation when Eastern Meditation was brought to English speaking countries. In doing so, however, the translators have deprived many Christians of a valuable tool for prayer.

In Eastern Meditation, the goal is to empty and quiet the mind. In Western Meditation, quieting the mind is only the process we go through to get to our goal. Our goal in Western Meditation is fostering a relationship, a closer relationship, with God. We are allowing God space to guide us in understanding our studies and deepening our prayers. These two forms of meditation may look the same to observers and preparation may be similar, but they are very different in fact.

I am not discouraging you from practicing Eastern Meditation forms which have a proven place in religious and medical circles. I'm merely pointing out they have a different focus. For the purposes of this book, we will be concentrating on Western Meditation forms.

Steps for Meditation:

- Keep paper, pen/pencil, and art materials close at hand.
- If you are under a time constraint, set a timer (preferably one that doesn't tick!) so you will not be distracted by watching the clock. I find a small, inexpensive, digital time works well for this. If you are using a meditation CD, the length of the CD will have the same effect.
- Offer a short prayer to God, stating your intention for this time of meditation. This is the time you will ask the question that is resting on your heart or request enlightenment on the scripture or study passage which concerns you.
- Sit quietly, concentrating on your breath. You might increase your focus by counting your breaths, counting to 5 as you inhale and 8 as you exhale. Some people use a physical object such as a candle or favorite picture as their focus. I began with

meditation CDs. Choose carefully what you decide to use for your meditation prompt. A candle is difficult to travel with and lighting one on a plane is frowned upon. Learning to focus using breath is portable and easy to use anywhere.

- Respond to the question, text, or study passage by reading with a centered focus on your breathing. You may need to pause occasionally to center again on your breathing. While not necessary, it is easier to meditate with your eyes closed to minimize distractions. If you have lots of noise in your environment, you might try using a meditation CD. Some are suggested in the Bibliography

- Write down any inspiration you may receive. While I have heard the still small voice directing me, teaching me, that is not the usual form the Lord's response takes. Generally, inspiration comes as a gentle nudging to do something, or a reminder of something I had not thought of in a long time. You may be directed to look up words for more nuances of meaning or receive a picture in your mind's eye you would want to sketch. You may even be directed to other scriptures or stories to boost your understanding. Sometimes, I've been directed to contact someone and ask my question. These kinds of direction happen to me frequently when I am stuck while preparing for a sermon.

- You may be directed to another prayer form – Lectio Divina, Walking Meditation, or Visualization Practice. If so, just transition smoothly into the other practice.

- When you sense the meditation is complete (or your timer goes off), sit quietly for the space of two breaths and express gratitude for the time you have shared with God. Then stretch and open your eyes.

## *Contemplation - Contemplatio:*

Contemplation has been practiced from the early days of Christianity. There is evidence that Jesus practiced both meditation and contemplation. The early Christian desert fathers practiced it constantly.

In all of the other prayer forms, we are involved. We are conscious of what is happening and have some control over the direction of the prayer. In Contemplation, this is not true.

Contemplation comes closer to Eastern Meditation than any other prayer form in Christianity. However, just as in Western Meditation, our goal is not about emptying our minds so much as it is about deepening a relationship with God. The brain-wave length for Contemplation is just a step above the Delta waves experienced in sleep. You may even fall asleep during Contemplation so you might want to set a timer. When you have experienced true Contemplation, you will know you were not asleep. However, I have found the effect to be just as powerful if I fall asleep during Contemplation as it would be if I had stayed awake.

In Contemplation, we let God take control. We release our control over ourselves and let God take over. Essentially, we are offering what we are to the Great Potter's hands; then letting the Spirit work while shutting down our imagination and reason; letting the Spirit work its miracle in our lives with groans and sighs too deep for words. We sit and listen.

When you first begin to Contemplate, you might want to try a CD to bring you into focus until you learn what that focus feels like. Once you know how it feels to experience Contemplation, it is easier to do the next time. Another help for Contemplation is to not try to quiet your thoughts completely. Just observe the thoughts that come up and let them go without getting hooked into them. Like a mountain observing a stream at its base, let the thoughts flow on past you. Like lying on your back watching clouds drift by, let the thoughts float by without engaging them. Eventually, they will quiet themselves when they realize you aren't listening.

Contemplation requires great faith for we are letting God "mess with" our inmost self, trusting that it will work for our good. We may see no change in ourselves at first, but the longer we practice, the more we will notice subtle changes: that irritating co-worker no longer irritates you; you don't react as angrily in traffic; you have more patience with your child then you once had.

It is a powerful meditation form and I encourage you to incorporate it into your prayer practices.

Steps for Contemplation are similar to those of Meditation:

- Keep paper and pen/pencils close at hand. You will not be making notes as you did in Meditation. This is for those chores that rise up to distract you. You will not be so tempted to get up and do them if you can write down a reminder.

- If you are under a time constraint or concerned about falling asleep, set a timer (preferably one that doesn't tick!) so you will not be distracted by watching the clock. If you are using a CD, the length of the CD will have the same effect.

- Offer a short prayer to God, stating your intention for this time of contemplation. You can request assistance with something specific you have been unsuccessful in addressing yourself.

- Sit quietly, concentrating on your breath. You might increase your focus by counting your breaths, counting to 5 as you inhale and 8 as you exhale. Some people use a physical object such as a candle or favorite picture as their focus. I began with meditation CDs. Choose carefully what you decide to use for your meditation prompt. A candle is difficult to travel with and lighting one on a plane is frowned upon. Learning to focus using breath is portable and easy to use anywhere.

- When you sense the Contemplation is complete (or your timer goes off), sit quietly for the space of two breaths and express gratitude towards God for your time together. Then stretch and open your eyes. Sit quietly for a moment longer to reorient yourself to your space.

- Write down any inspiration or insights you may have received. Do not be concerned if you don't have any to write down. The focus of Contemplation is the adjustment and healing of the sub-conscious. Only daily journaling or awareness of your life responses will document the effects of Contemplation on your daily life.

At first, it may not seem like anything is happening. However, after taking three classes in Contemplation simultaneously one summer, requiring one half hour of daily Contemplation apiece in addition to what we practiced in class, I found myself contemplating a total of 4.5 hours/per day. I experienced a huge drop in my stress levels, a huge increase in my patience and ability to ignore minor offenses such as being cut-off in traffic. Most profound of all, my regular prayer times seemed to become more important and more powerful.

## *Consciousness Examen*

In the Consciousness Examen, we work with the Holy Spirit to find what needs to be set straight in our lives. We can specifically work on a habit that needs changing, something that we have done (maybe without realizing it) for which we need forgiveness or something that we need to forgive. The Consciousness Examen can also be used to grow closer to God or to get rid of anything that might be separating us from God. It will also help us become more aware of our lives so that they do not pass by mindlessly or unexamined.

The Examen should be performed daily just before going to bed or first thing each morning. It can also be practiced in conjunction with any of the other prayer forms.

Always approach the Examen with an attitude of humility and determination to act on whatever is brought to your mind. In this way, your session will become more and more productive as the Spirit responds to your sincerity.

The steps of the Examen are as follows:

- Withdraw into a quiet space and meditate silently in preparation for the response of the Spirit. You should develop an attitude of mind that wills the healing of any problem the Spirit presents to you. If you are practicing the Examen with an expressed purpose in mind, review that purpose now.

- Ask quietly for the Holy Spirit to bring into your awareness any of the day's activities you need to notice. You may begin this portion by performing a short run-through of the highlights of your day, holding each up to the Spirit's light. You can also divide your day into smaller parts such as hourly segments. Or use the Visualize Meditation and see your day as a movie, or small, puffy clouds floating by in a blue sky, or a slow moving river with toy sailboats floating past, or even a train with each car a segment of your day, all of which can be stopped when the Spirit brings your focus on that segment. The idea is to see your day through God's eyes.

- When anything is brought to your attention, examine it carefully, and prayerfully. Why is your attention being focused on this particular event? Analyze the elements: What was the incident? How did it begin? How did it end?

- Work with the Spirit to determine what, if anything, you need to do about this situation. Do you need to ask God or anybody else for forgiveness? Do you need to forgive? Is it something you just need to remember or something you need to pray about right now?

- Is it a habit or situation you are trying to change? Is there any way to prevent this situation from happening again? How might you act differently? Respond differently? Ask the Spirit to intervene in your actions the next time this situation occurs. It could be a request for a gentle prodding to remind you of this intervention or a request to slow down the situation so that you can realize what is happening and stop the cycle.

- Record what has transpired in your journal. This record will be helpful when you get discouraged. It will show you how far you've come. Thank the Holy Spirit for helping you draw closer to God. Sit quietly for a moment before leaving the meditation.

Here is an example of a prompt requiring immediate action. A woman in a class I was teaching wanted to bond more closely with her family. She began practicing the Consciousness Examen every evening before going to bed, asking God to show her opportunities to connect with a family member she may have missed. She settled into her prayer space and almost immediately, she was reminded of her 7-year-old son trying to tell her something four or five times during the course of the evening. Each time she had been too busy. He had even tried again as she was tucking him in, but she told him to go to sleep and they would talk about it in the morning. Accompanying this memory was an urgent prodding to go talk to him right then and not wait until morning. She went to his room, sure that he was asleep. He was not asleep. In fact, he was sobbing. She took him in her arms, apologized for not listening to him sooner, and asked him what he wanted to tell her. In their classroom at school, the kids took turns bringing a snack for their quiet time in the afternoon. Tomorrow was his turn and he needed to bring two dozen cookies in the morning! She immediately got him up and they shared some hot cocoa as they fixed slice and bake cookies and boxed them up for the morning. The reminder had done just what the Consciousness Examen is supposed to do. It brought her closer to her son and saved her from a hectic, stress-filled morning.

## Praying the Lord's Prayer

This approach to prayer prays the Lord's Prayer, not as a prayer in itself, but as a template for prayer.

The best way to approach this prayer is to set a time limit for each section. That way you will go through the entire prayer with time for listening as well as speaking. If you are strict with yourself by limiting the time for each section of the prayer, the prayer can be even more powerful. (Going longer in a section is okay, but do not shorten any section.) If you take five minutes for each section of the prayer, you will have prayed for 45 minutes. Three minutes for each section will take you almost 30 minutes. I know this seems like a lot of time if you are struggling to pray even five minutes a day, but it will not seem like a lot of time while you are involved in the prayer, especially if you are only spending three minutes per section.

Try to take some time for listening during each part of the prayer. After a couple of weeks of practice, you may discover that God has more to say to you than you have to say to God.

This prayer format may seem like a very logical and structured way to pray, but it can be very powerful if approached with reverence for the intention of the prayer, which is spending time with God on a daily basis.

The following will assist you in understanding the focus of each section:

- At the beginning of each section, set your timer for the length of time you decided to pray each section. This will prevent the distraction of watching the time.

- "Our Father, who art in heaven, hallowed be Thy name" – This is a time for praising God. Sing a hymn to yourself or recite a psalm. Write a psalm or some other form of poem, chant, or prose. Resting silently in the presence of nature can also be a form of praise.

- "Thy Kingdom come" – This part of your prayer is a prayer for the coming of Zion, the peaceable Kingdom, or the Kingdom of God on earth. A prayer for our missionaries and church planters as well as the leadership of the church would be called for at this point. Prayer for an upcoming World or national event could be included here. It would also be helpful to ask God to lead you to notice others in need during the day.

- "Thy Will be done on earth as it is in heaven." – Here is a prayer for God's will to be done in your life. Just as you prayed for God's will to be done on the earth in the above section, so you are now praying that God's will be done inside you as well. At first, this section could be a difficult prayer for you since it may include some repentance on your part, but it will be powerful if prayed on a daily basis.

- "Give us this day our daily bread" – This is the place for intercessory prayer on behalf of yourself and others. Pray what is resting on your heart this day and ask that your prayers may be in accordance with God's will. The more time you spend in God's presence, the more your heart will be expanded, and your will align with God's. Giving thanks for answered prayer would be appropriate at this point. This is why keeping a Prayer Request journal is important. Not only to help you remember the people, situations, and things you pray for, but it also helps you notice when your prayers are answered.

- "Forgive us our debts" – Ask God to show you anything in your life that is less than His standards for you. If nothing comes to mind, sit in silent meditation, listening until the allotted time is up. Something you have resisted examining may be able to surface then. Using the Consciousness Examen as a tool here is very helpful.

- "As we forgive our debtors" – Now ask God to show you anything for which you need to forgive somebody. If nothing comes to mind, sit in silent meditation, listening until the allotted time is up. Something you have resisted examining may be able to surface then. Again, the Consciousness Examen is a good tool here.

- "Suffer us not to be led into temptation, but deliver us from evil" – This is a prayer for our day. It asks God to go into our day with us that we may enter it, trusting the Spirit's guidance, and calling on God's interference should we be less than we can be. It is a prayer for spiritual defense. It is also a prayer for discernment that all decisions may be made with the Spirit's guidance.

- "For Thine is the Kingdom, and the Power and the Glory forever and ever" – Ending with praise is a powerful way to go forth from a prayer. It ends the prayer and begins (or ends) the day on a joyous note. Once again turn to the psalms, a hymn, or rest in nature. Listen to a praise song. Start a gratitude journal and write in it daily.

- "Amen" – This word is Greek for "so be it." It makes all that came before a statement of fact. It is an acknowledgment of faith in God and God's ability to influence your world. Sit for the allotted time reflecting on the fact that God, the Creator of the Universe, just took time to hear you. Now listen. Does God have anything else to say to you?

Jesus' teaching on prayer is very powerful. Practice each morning for a couple of weeks to give yourself a chance to get into the routine and understand the process completely before judging its effectiveness in your life.

## *Lectio Divina or The Divine Word*

There will come a time during your prayer life when you will want a deeper understanding of scripture. Lectio Divina is a prayer supporting such a desire. The poet, Macrina Wiederkehr, O.S.B., in her book, A Tree Full of Angels, calls it the "golden prayer."

Lectio Divina is not a programmed 1-2-3-4 sequence though it is taught that way. Prayer is a gift and Lectio is meant to help us respond to that gift and prepare ourselves for its further development. The "timetable" is not our own. We may find ourselves flowing through the sequence only to come out of the Meditation flow with more questions that take us back to the Reading section. Or we may complete the Contemplation section realizing we need to revisit the scripture through Meditation on something that came up as a result of Contemplation.

Begin with a prayer for the guidance of the Holy Spirit. Then move into the scripture as follows:

- Prayer for guidance
- Reading - Lectio:
    - Quiet the body and mind, then choose a text, preferably a short one.
    - Read it slowly, out loud if possible, while carefully listening. You may want to read it three times through.
    - Personalize the text as if God were speaking to you.
    - When a passage, phrase, or word captures your attention, stay with it and move into Meditation
- Meditation - Meditatio:
    - Respond to the text by rereading at a deeper level the phrase or word that caught your attention.
    - Look up words for more nuances of meaning.
    - If it's a story, you might try using Visualization Practice to put yourself into the story. Dwell on the scripture passage quietly, turning it over in your mind. However you feel guided to do it, let the scripture move you.

- o   After a few minutes or as you feel ready, move on to the prayer section.
- Prayer - Oratio:
  - o   This is not something to do, but a prayer of the heart.
  - o   Let your prayer begin orally if necessary, but let it express what you discovered during the meditation.
  - o   Let the longing of your heart take over whether in words, tears, or simply an unnamed longing.
  - o   As you feel ready, move on to Contemplation.
- Contemplation - Contemplatio:
  - o   In the other three areas, we were involved in some activity. In this stage, we move to a deeper level in relationship to God. We let God take control. We release our control over the relationship and let God take over, offering what we are to the Great Potter's hands. We shut off our imagination and reason, letting the Spirit work its miracle in our lives.—We sit and listen.
  - o   If you have trouble quieting your mind, just observe the thoughts without getting hooked by them. Like a mountain observing a stream at its base, let the thoughts flow on past you. Eventually, they will quiet themselves when they realize you aren't listening.
  - o   This step requires great faith in that we are letting God "mess with" our inmost self, trusting that it will work for our good.
- Prayer of Gratitude
  - o   Whatever route your prayer has taken, whether direct or repeating certain sections, end your prayer time with a prayer of gratitude.
  - o   This prayer is an acknowledgement of God's mercy and grace in taking this time with you. Feel this gratitude with humility and understanding of this great honor.

It would be good at the end of this time to write down what you have learned during the prayer or any observations you might have. This prayer is very quiet, and its effects on our lives are gradual and gentle. It is only in retrospect that we realize that we have been changed into fuller beings that are closer to the example Christ has set for us.

## The Jesus Prayer (also known as "Prayer of the Heart")

This prayer integrates the following five elements:

- The name of Jesus
- The desire for God's mercy and healing presence
- Continual repetition of a word or short phrase from scripture
- Awareness of the body, especially the rhythm of breath or heartbeat
- Recognition that God cannot be known with words; God is encountered in silence

The Jesus Prayer is also known as the Prayer of the Heart. Rather than praying with just our heads, the prayer of the heart seeks to engage the whole human person in prayer. By repeating a phrase from scripture over and over, the practitioner bypasses the distracting activity of mental prayer by engaging in a form of self-hypnosis in order to commune with God in the quiet inner places of our beings.

It is an important prayer because we frequently try to formulate a string of words to get some point across to God. But when we pray only with the mind, or intellect, we pray with only a fragment of our whole self. When we pray with the heart, we pray with all of our being. We offer all we are in the hope of divine encounter.

In the Judeo-Christian tradition, the heart is not just the center of our emotional life. Biblically, the word "heart" refers to the whole person – it is the coordinating center that integrates mind, body, emotions, will, and moral choices. That is the place deep within us where human and divine meet. That is the place for our prayer to take root in God.

*The Unforgivable Sin*

The first Jesus prayer was uttered by the beggar, Bartimaeus, as a prayer for healing. Jesus heard him and healed his blindness. When we pray with the heart, with the whole self, we seek healing for the whole person. It is important to note: The healing we receive will be the healing God sees we need. It will not necessarily be a physical healing.

If the heart encompasses ALL aspects of who we are as a person, then it also extends beyond our immediate self to include our relationships with others. When we pray with the heart, we are praying not only for ourselves but for those we carry in our hearts – our family, our friends, and colleagues, casual acquaintances or even persons unknown to us with whom we are, nevertheless, intimately connected. Indeed, praying with the heart in the space where God is always present, is praying for the world.

Some scripture passages that birthed the Jesus Prayer are:

- "Pray without ceasing!" – 1 Thessalonians 5:17
- "Bartimaeus son of Timaeus, a blind beggar was sitting by the roadside. When he heard that it was Jesus of Nazareth, he began to shout out and say, 'Jesus, Son of David, have mercy on me.' Many sternly ordered him to be quiet, but he cried out even more loudly, 'Son of David, have mercy on me!' Jesus stood still and said, 'Call him here.' And they called the blind man, saying to him, 'Take heart; get up, he is calling you.'" – Mark 10:46-52
- "…the mystery that has been hidden throughout the ages and generations but has now been revealed to his saints. To them God chose to make known how great among the Gentiles are the riches of the glory of this mystery, which is Christ in you, the hope of glory." –Colossians 1:26-27
- "Likewise the Spirit helps us in our weakness; for we do not know how to pray as we ought, but that very Spirit intercedes with sighs too deep for words. And God, who searches the heart, knows what is the mind of the Spirit, because the Spirit intercedes for the saints according to the will of God." --Romans 8:26-27

To practice the prayer, follow this format:

- Before you begin, choose which version of the Jesus Prayer feels right for you.
    - The traditional form of the Jesus Prayer appropriates the petition of the beggar on the road to Jericho, "Lord Jesus Christ (or Savior), Son of the Living God (or Son of David), have mercy on me, a sinner."
    - Shorter phrases that focus on the name of Jesus and the desire for God's mercy may be more appropriate. They capture the essence of the prayer while being more easily adapted to the rhythm of one's breathing: "Lord Jesus Christ have mercy on me," or "Jesus, Son of David, have mercy on me," or "Jesus, have mercy on me"
    - Simply invoking the name "Jesus" or single words such as "peace" or "mercy" are excellent alternatives, as well.
- Find a comfortable prayer-meditation position. Let your breathing become relaxed and easy. Without forcing it, allow the rhythm of your breath to slow gradually and deepen. By paying attention to your breath, you promote a quiet, interior awareness. It is important to use the breath as you begin this prayer because the prayer is meant to be carried into the world with you as you will soon see.
- Let the word or words you have selected for your prayer take form in your mind. You might imagine yourself looking into your heart, then carrying your thoughts from your head down into your heart.
- Gradually fit the words of the prayer to the natural rhythm of your breath. For example, internally say the words "Lord Jesus Christ" as you inhale and "have mercy on me" as you exhale. Alternatively, you might breathe in with silence, then mentally utter the prayer phrase with each breath out. You can also try softly vocalizing the words if you have trouble concentrating.

- Remember, this prayer is not intended for rational analysis of content and words. Refrain as best you can from having a conversation with yourself about the words you are saying, their meaning for your life, and so on. That is part of the conversation you had with yourself as you selected the word or words.

- Once the Jesus prayer establishes itself in your heart you may find, like other practitioners of the prayer have reported, that the prayer will begin to "pray itself" inside you. The words invoking the name of Jesus and God's compassionate presence may spontaneously surface as you go about your daily tasks. You may find yourself repeating them as you do your shopping or while you wait at a stoplight. They may even come to inhabit your dreams. Then you will be praying "without ceasing"; then the Spirit will be praying for you. Praying without ceasing is the goal of this prayer.

- Continue silently praying the Jesus Prayer for a minimum of five to ten minutes or do as the desert fathers who developed this prayer and recite it a certain number of times each day. They began by praying the prayer 100 times per day the first week. The next week the repetitions would increase to 1000 times per day. The next week 2000 times per day. They would increase with each week until the repetitions reached 10,000 times per day. At this point, the prayer has established itself in your mind and you will indeed be "praying always."

## *Write a letter*

Do not allow this letter to be a substitute for face-to-face forgiveness or repentance statements when such things are possible. It is only to be used when circumstances will not allow for a face-to-face statement. It definitely is not a substitute for restitution.

- Tell the story of your injury or the injury you caused as well as all the effect it has had on you, your family, and your life. Include anything even remotely attached to the circumstances (the ripple effect).

- Finish the letter with a paragraph that is a prayer to God to help you forgive or repent and release this incident. Place it in God's hands.
- Place it in a secure location to let it rest for 24 hours.
- The next day, as part of a prayer reread the letter. Add anything you left off in the original writing.
- Once you have reread the letter and you are satisfied it contains all you need to say, pray the closing prayer of the letter with a desire to be free of or reduce for the other the pain and anger related to the instance. Say, "I release this into God's hands." as you destroy the letter.

There is only one time such a letter would be delivered: when the situation has created a rift with a loved one and you cannot locate the person, you could leave it with someone you know the loved one might contact to find you. A woman I know who was dying of cancer had only one regret; she would not be able to make up with her estranged daughter before she died because she could not find her. She wrote a letter to her daughter and left it with her mother, the girl's grandmother. She knew her daughter was still close to her grandmother. This way, should her daughter want to reconcile, she would know her mother still loved her. The woman was then able to die in peace.

## *Using Artwork*

This exercise is especially good if you do not understand how you are feeling, or you are a visual person. Collage, painting, sculpting, creating altars from found objects as you walk: all of these things have a place in prayer and worship.

For instance, I am not a very visual person, but drawing mandalas (basically, a circle on a piece of paper) is perfect for helping me understand my feelings about a situation and add depth to my prayers. The circle is used as a centering device for your thoughts and emotions about the event. The process I follow when using the mandala is:

*The Unforgivable Sin*

- Do not use the pre-drawn mandalas in coloring books or try to make a specific picture or even stay in the lines unless that is the direction your feelings are leading you. This exercise is a picture of your emotional response to the situation and may or may not incorporate actual drawings of things. If you are not artistically inclined, it doesn't matter. You are the only one who needs to see it.

- Take crayons, colored pencils, paints, or markers and a piece of paper (preferably drawing or watercolor paper), draw a circle that fills most of the center of the page. You might even try finger paints

- Sit in silent prayer for a moment, then let your feelings loose..

- Get your feelings out there, even if it means cutting or tearing the paper to give them expression.

- When you are finished, sit quietly, praying with the results. You may want to journal or jot down on a piece of paper whatever comes to you—new insights or actions you need to take to set yourself free or make restitution for your actions.

- You may want to treat this as the letter in the letter exercise and say "I release this into God's hands." as you destroy the mandala.

## *Movement Meditations*

Movement Meditations encompasses a whole range of activities. Included as movement meditations are walking labyrinths, practicing Tai Chi or Yoga, any repetitive exercise including running, or just taking a walk.

- Go alone. Unless you have a trusted friend, minister, Spiritual Director, or family member who understands and is committed to the process of keeping silence, it is easier to listen and release if you are alone.

- At the start of your activity, establish your transformation point. Decide on the duration of the activity. If you are walking or running, set a destination. Establish the halfway point to finish rehearsing all the issues prompting the prayer. If you are walking a labyrinth, it would be the center of the labyrinth. If you are practicing yoga or Tai Chi, it would be the half way point of your practice time.

- When you reach the target point or halfway point, pause to pray about what you have just reviewed. Pray for release.

- As you continue your activity, pray for the ability to forgive or repent of each issue that came to you on your journey to the transformation point. Let yourself feel each issue either detaching itself from you and being left behind or plans for restitution you may wish to make. You may want to take bread crumbs or small stones with you so you can drop them as a symbol of your release.

## *Gratitude Practice*

The Gratitude Practice may seem to be a repetition of the section on the Gratitude Journal. However, this is a more spontaneous response to the blessings of God. You don't necessarily need to keep a journal to do this. What you need is a heart filled with praise.

- When you are feeling down or despairing, look for something to be thankful for. If you can't think of anything because you are so downhearted, pray for something to be brought to your mind. This is also important to do when you are confronted with something amazing.

- Meditate on what it is about the thing making you so happy and joyous. Let your mind linger in that amazing, wonderful space. Enjoy the moment. Make it clear to yourself why you are thankful for these things.

- Open your heart in praise and thanksgiving before God. Recite a Psalm or phrase that comes to mind. Sing a hymn. Shout to the Lord. Murmur a quiet prayer of gratitude.

- Reflect on how the form your gratitude took supported your spirit of gratitude.
- End the moment with meditation on the greatness of God.

Gratitude may seem to have nothing to do with repentance or forgiveness, or it may appear to be just a Pollyanna-type of exercise, but it takes your eyes off of your issues or needs and puts them on God. It raises your spirits. It is also an act of obedience. 1 Thessalonians 5:16-18 tells us to:

> *"Rejoice always, pray without ceasing, give thanks in all circumstances; for this is the will of God in Christ Jesus for you."*

By obeying God in one thing, we open ourselves to obeying God in other things.

## Visualization Practice

The imagination is a tool given us by God to augment our ability to spiritually discern the realm of God. I Corinthians 2:14-16 tells us this:

> *"Those who are unspiritual do not receive the gifts of God's Spirit, for they are foolishness to them, and they are unable to understand them because they are spiritually discerned. Those who are spiritual discern all things, and they are themselves subject to no one else's scrutiny. For who has known the mind of the Lord so as to instruct him? But we have the mind of Christ."*

While we are cautioned not to use the imagination for evil and vain things, we are repeatedly told to discern the will of God. Many times this can only be done by using the imagination.

Jesus used his imagination to invoke ours through parables. He made up stories to teach us the things difficult to explain in any other way. The Scriptures take up this same idea. They tell us who Jesus is by sharing stories about him: showing instead of telling.

One of the easiest ways to understand these stories is to imagine ourselves to be part of the story. We allow the Spirit to assign us our part in the story. For instance, I have had difficulties with the story of Mary and Martha, the one where Jesus claims Mary has chosen the better part. When I allowed myself to be put into the story by the Spirit, I found myself as a maid helping Martha with all the work. Martha was affronted by Jesus' words. She felt all her hard work was unappreciated by the man she most respected and for whom she was working. I could relate to this from personal experience with people I worked for. But I saw something else. Jesus came to Martha afterwards, expressed His appreciation for her work, but now was the time for Him to share His work with her. Martha joined him then, and invited us to do the same.

How do you do this? It is very easy:

- Read the story you are wanting to study until you have the basics memorized. I especially like to do this with stories I find problematic, like the one with Martha and Mary above.
- Sit quietly, concentrating on your breath. Take three deep breaths and let them out, slowly.
- On the last breath, ask Jesus or the Holy Spirit to go with you into the story so you may obtain a better understanding of the circumstances and the message.
- Begin to construct the scene of the story in your mind. If you are not a visual person, construct the story the way it might have sounded, felt, tasted, or smelled. In the story above, I saw the kitchen with all the noise of dishes clattering, cooking pots, washing up, frequent calls for clean towels and water for washing the feet of guests still coming, the neighbor women bringing extra bread and then staying to help…and the transition as I carried trays of food and drink into the room where Jesus was speaking to the guests. Think about not just the sights, but also the smells, the sounds, and the silences.
- Then: Action. In the story above, the action began with Martha and me bringing in more food and Jesus speaking. Then Martha sees Mary just sitting there entranced with the full pitcher of

water she was supposed to be using to fill the foot-washing basins. And Martha begins.

- Let the action play itself out. Notice everything. What are the sounds around you? What do you smell, if anything? What feelings do you have?
- When the action completes, sit quietly inside the story, breathing lightly, until you are ready to come out of it.
- Write down your insights. Perhaps ask yourself some of the following questions:
    - What part was I assigned in the story? Was I an observer, or the main character? Why was that important for my understanding of the story?
    - What new insights did I receive from the story?
    - Do I have a new feeling of sympathy for the participants in the story? Perhaps a deeper understanding of their turmoil and struggle?
    - How do these mirror my own understandings of my life and the people around me? For instance, I am a Mary person, but my mother is a Martha person. It helped me understand some of our frustrations with each other as I grew up. I understood Jesus came to teach the women as well as the men.
- When you have carefully and prayerfully evaluated the story for all it can give you, take three slow, deep breaths and come back to yourself.

That's it! Simple, yet profound. When I've used this with stories I've known since childhood, they have given me new insights into my faith, my relationships with others, and with God.

# Bibliography

**Books:**

Bell, Rob, *Love Wins: A Book About Heaven, Hell, and the Fate of Every Person Who Ever Lived*, New York: HarperCollins Publishers, 2005.

Keating, Thomas, *Open Mind, Open Heart: The Contemplative Dimension of the Gospel*, 20th Anniversary ed., N.Y.: The Continuum International Publishing Group Inc., 2006.

Merton, Thomas, *Seeds of Contemplation*, New York: New Directions Publishing Corporation, 1986.

*Philokalia: The Eastern Christian Spiritual Texts-Selections Annotated & Explained*. Annotated & Explained by Allyne Smith. Translated by G.E.H. Palmer, Philip Sherrard, and Bishop Kallistos Ware. Woodstock, VT, Skylight Paths Publishing, 2010.

Progoff Ph.D, Ira, *At a Journal Workshop: Writing to Access the Power of the Unconscious and Evoke Creative Ability*, New York: Penguin Putnam Inc, 1992.

Rohr, Richard, *The Divine Dance: The Trinity and Your Transformation*, New Kensington, PA: Whitaker House, 2016.

Roth, Gabrielle, *Sweat Your Prayers: Movement as Spiritual Practice*, New York: Penguin Putnam Inc, 1997.

Wiederkehr, Macrina, *A Tree Full of Angels: Seeing the Holy in the Ordinary,* New York: HarperCollins Publishers, 1990.

**Meditation Music**

There are many musical resources for meditation. These are some I have used.

Bach, Johann Sebastian, *Bach for Relaxation*, a variety of artists and instruments, RCAVictor.

Gordon, David & Steve, *Drum Medicine*, Sequoia Records, compact sound disc, drumming, flute, nature sounds.

Gordon, David & Steve, *Sacred Spirit Drums*, Sequoia Records, compact sound disc, drumming, flute, nature sounds.

Mozart, Wolfgang Amadeus, *The Mozart Effect: Vol II-Music for Rest & Relaxation*, Compiled and Sequenced by Don Campbell, Spring Hill Music.

Mozart, Wolfgang Amadeus, *The Mozart Effect: Vol V-Music for Rest & Rejuvenation*, Compiled and Sequenced by Don Campbell, Spring Hill Music.

Thompson, Dr. Jeffrey, *Alpha Relaxation System*, The Relaxation Company, compact sound disc.

Thompson, Dr. Jeffrey, *Delta Sleep System*, The Relaxation Company, compact sound disc.

Thompson, Dr. Jeffrey, *Gamma Meditation System 2.0*, The Relaxation Company, compact sound disc.

Thompson, Dr. Jeffrey, *Theta Meditation System*, The Relaxation Company, compact sound disc.

Van Sickle, Kurt, *Make Me An Instrument*, Isun Music, 7003-CD. Compact sound disc. Chant, also a good accompaniment for Tai Chi Chih.

# About the Author

Mikal J. Shedd is a Minister of Blessing in the Community of Christ. She has had several unlooked for mystical experiences which are frequently referred to in her writings. Her way of being in the world builds its foundation on daily prayer, scripture study, and powerful experiences of God's presence.

She holds a Bachelor's Degree in Business Administration from Wayne State College, Wayne, NE and worked as an accountant for 40+ years. She holds a Bachelor's Degree in Religious Studies from the University of Nebraska-Omaha and a Masters in Christian Spirituality from Creighton University. She has been described by family as dependable but unpredictable; and as a creative accountant, but in a good way.

Rev. Shedd has ministered in various priesthood offices in Community of Christ since the mid-1980s. She has been called to serve her church as a Bishop over a jurisdiction including Kansas City, Missouri and Salina and Wichita, Kansas. Her current calling to Minister of Blessing is a challenging call to be present with God for the people wherever she finds herself.

Rev. Shedd brings spiritual formation into a focused and usable format. She believes all people are called to a mystical connection with God. Her way of connecting is through the Christian path of the Trinity. She writes in the hopes of people finding the blessings of Christ available to them through a more conscious and closer awareness of a loving presence in their lives so they will live in peace with their families and neighbors.

CPSIA information can be obtained
at www.ICGtesting.com
Printed in the USA
FFHW021649170119
50187157-55152FF